T0318901

Cambridge Elements

Elements in Development Economics
Series Editor-in-Chief
Kunal Sen
UNU-WIDER and University of Manchester

SURVIVAL OF THE GREENEST

Economic Transformation in a Climate-conscious World

Amir Lebdioui
University of Oxford

CAMBRIDGE
UNIVERSITY PRESS

Shaftesbury Road, Cambridge CB2 8EA, United Kingdom

One Liberty Plaza, 20th Floor, New York, NY 10006, USA

477 Williamstown Road, Port Melbourne, VIC 3207, Australia

314–321, 3rd Floor, Plot 3, Splendor Forum, Jasola District Centre, New Delhi – 110025, India

103 Penang Road, #05–06/07, Visioncrest Commercial, Singapore 238467

Cambridge University Press is part of Cambridge University Press & Assessment, a department of the University of Cambridge.

We share the University's mission to contribute to society through the pursuit of education, learning and research at the highest international levels of excellence.

www.cambridge.org
Information on this title: www.cambridge.org/9781009500517

DOI: 10.1017/9781009339414

First published 2024

A catalogue record for this publication is available from the British Library.

ISBN 978-1-009-50051-7 Hardback
ISBN 978-1-009-33938-4 Paperback
ISSN 2755-1601 (online)
ISSN 2755-1598 (print)

Survival of the Greenest

Economic Transformation in a Climate-conscious World

Elements in Development Economics

DOI: 10.1017/9781009339414
First published online: April 2024

Amir Lebdioui
University of Oxford

Author for correspondence: Amir Lebdioui, amirlebdioui@gmail.com

Abstract: The pathways to economic development are changing. Environmental sustainability is no longer a choice but a necessity to maintain a competitive edge in the global economy. Just like in nature, where survival hinges on adaptation, this Element shows how nations adjust to – and take advantage of – the new dynamics of structural transformation induced by climate change. First, by analysing the uneven industrial geography of decarbonisation, the inadequate state of climate financing, and the rise of green protectionism, it demonstrates that the low-carbon economy stands to increase economic disparities between nations unless action is taken. Then, by examining green industrial policies and their varied success, it explains how governments can still join the green industrialisation race. Finally, it examines how to adapt green industrial policy to different starting points, market sizes, productive structures, state–business relations dynamics, institutional layouts, and ecological contexts. This title is also available as Open Access on Cambridge Core.

Keywords: economic development, climate change, sustainability, industrial policy, structural change

ISBNs: 9781009500517 (HB), 9781009339384 (PB), 9781009339414 (OC)
ISSNs: 2755-1601 (online), 2755-1598 (print)

Contents

1 Introduction: A Changing Climate for Economic
  Development   1

2 Rethinking Resilience to Climate and Transition Risks and
  the Role of Productive Diversification   12

3 Industrial Opportunities Arising Out of Low-Carbon
  Transitions: Who Benefits?   18

4 Governments as Referees and Head Coaches: The
  Political Economy of Green Industrial Policy   26

5 No Green Silver Bullets: Various Pathways to Green
  Industrialisation beyond Manufacturing   48

6 Kicking Away the 'Green' Ladder: Green Protectionism,
  Broken Pledges, and Double Trade Standards   63

7 Conclusion and Reflections on the Future Relevance
  of Development Economics   70

References   74

1 Introduction: A Changing Climate for Economic Development

> It is not the most intellectual of the species that survives; it is not the strongest that survives; but the species that survives is the one that is able best to adapt and adjust to the changing environment in which it finds itself.
>
> — Charles Darwin

From the simplest organisms to the most complex ecosystems, the ability to evolve in response to environmental changes has been the cornerstone of survival, including for humans. This principle of adaptation in the natural world finds a compelling parallel in the realm of economics. As we navigate the twenty-first century, it becomes increasingly evident that economic development strategies, much like biological species, must adapt to respond to a growingly vital concern for climate change, which stands out as one of the most important existential threats that humanity has faced. Globally, the past seven years have been the seven warmest years on record since 1850 (World Meteorological Organization, 2021a). There is a scientific consensus that if global temperature increases by 2 °C, 37 per cent of the world population will be exposed to severe (and often deadly) heatwaves at least once every five years; while sea-level rise will lead to salinisation of water supplies and other impacts on ecological systems (Oppenheimer et al., 2019). Increased water scarcity will generate conflict, exacerbate poverty, population displacement, and famine. Even keeping temperatures from rising more than 1.5 °C above pre-industrial levels, as stipulated in the Paris climate agreement, entails harsh consequences, but makes the difference between a planet that's still suitable for humans to live on and one that is not.

Thanks to decades of research, we broadly know how to address climate change: by expanding low-carbon solutions, replacing fossil fuels with clean energies, and avoiding unsustainable overconsumption. However, what we still do *not* know is how to ensure economic prosperity and sustain livelihoods while decarbonising our planet. The dual agenda between economic development and decarbonisation has been the source of heated academic debates but remains poorly understood, especially in practice. This is partly why politicians are rarely inclined to jeopardise economic goals in favour of environmental ones. In poor countries, the dilemma is even more considerable: despite the progress achieved over the past century, extreme poverty (i.e. subsisting on less than USD 2.15/day) is still the reality for every tenth person in the world (around 648 million people, see World Bank, 2022), and is even expected to increase due to climate-induced shocks.[1]

---

[1] Meanwhile, 47 per cent of the world lives on less than USD 6.85 per day – a poverty line broadly reflective of the lines adopted in upper-middle income countries (World Bank, 2022).

Though they have not benefited from rising living standards on the back of highly polluting development models, developing countries disproportionately suffer from the economic consequences of climate change. Beyond its effects on GDP (which is misleading as an indicator of economic progress), climate change also disproportionately affects the export capacity of developing nations because most developing nations highly depend on the extraction of raw materials (especially agriculture and fossil fuels) as a source of exports, revenues, and jobs, which are highly vulnerable to both climate risks and transition risks (see Section 2).[2] Furthermore, global decarbonisation stands to increase economic disparities between countries, with the poorest nations being left – and perhaps even pushed – behind in the industrial geography of decarbonisation (see Section 3).

Against this backdrop, the optimal pathways to economic development are changing. The exact conditions that allowed nations to successfully industrialise and develop over the past century are not replicable – nor suitable – anymore. Carbon-intensive industrialisation models (which underpinned the East Asian miracle since the 1960s) present limits as well as blocked entry routes, not only due to the rise of China as an industrial powerhouse but also because those models are incompatible with the transition towards a low-carbon future. Notwithstanding the benefits that growth and industrialisation have brought millions of people – lifting them out of poverty, reducing infant mortality, and increasing life expectancy – evidence now shows that this approach has brought us to the brink of an ecological catastrophe, putting at serious risk all these benefits (Ekins and Zenghelis, 2021). Today, the growing sustainability agenda, changing consumer demand, the adoption of environmental regulations and sustainable trade standards, and the rise of carbon taxes imply that what has worked in the past will not work today.

So, what are the ways forward? Developing countries, having not used their share of the atmospheric stock of carbon, have a claim for the right to pollute. But is that necessarily the optimal course of action for local populations? Is industrial development still the optimal pathway to poverty reduction – and if so, what type of model can help reconcile industrialisation with sustainability? Is low-carbon manufacturing the only pathway to green economic transformation? For latecomers, is green industrialisation an easier route for catching up than standard industrialisation? What policy tools will help countries get there, especially those with limited pre-existing capabilities? Where is green industrial policy bearing positive outcomes, and what are the factors that

---

[2]　The ability to export is a critical feature of a country's economic development and prosperity (as it supports the accumulation of foreign exchange that can be used to finance the imports of factors of production).

influence its success? Are the international financial and trade systems supporting a just transition, or are they exacerbating the disparities in terms of green economic opportunities between rich and poor nations?

Answering such questions is no easy task, and this Element does not claim to provide all the answers. However, by exploring the various pathways to green economic transformation and their political economy underpinnings, I aim to explain how governments can overcome the important obstacles that stand in the way of a truly sustainable development. The core argument of this Element is that although countries seeking economic development would not benefit from replicating carbon-intensive economic strategies, industrial policy remains as relevant as ever in a low-carbon future. However, this industrial policy cannot reproduce errors of the past and needs to be based on new principles of ecological viability.

Beyond the 'Grow Now – Clean Up Later' Logic

Historically, the common approach to economic development in the context of sustainability has consisted of focusing on getting rich first and hoping to have the resources to fix the environment later (Ekins and Zenghelis, 2021). Recent evidence also suggests that industrialised nations with higher export sophistication have a higher ability to lower greenhouse gas (GHG) emissions (Romero and Gramkow, 2021), with considerable path dependence between manufacturing capabilities and low-carbon technologies. For instance, Brazil's pre-existing aerospace sector helped to develop a wind turbine industry (Hochstetler, 2020); Malaysia and China's existing electronics capabilities supported the domestic production of solar cells, while Norway's offshore oil production helped the country develop an offshore wind energy industry. Policymakers may also want to pursue the 'grow now, clean up later' strategy to wait until environmental solutions have been developed elsewhere and incremental improvements, learning by doing, and economies of scale have brought costs down, rather than incurring development costs themselves (Arrow, 1972; Guo & Fan, 2017). Lastly, delaying environmental action may also be preferred to avoid political resistance (Pegels and Altenburg, 2020).

However, this strategy presents severe limitations:

(1) Delaying action to embark on a green transformation implies high risks, not only of ecological damage but also of losses from asset stranding and lock-in in carbon-intensive economic, innovation, and institutional pathways, especially because energy systems are subject to long-lived path dependence (Aghion et al., 2019; Fouquet, 2016).

(2) Delaying greening can also incur extra costs of having to pursue more radical restructuring measures if they are delayed to the future (Acemoglu et al., 2012; Pegels and Altenburg, 2020; Stern, 2007).

(3) There is an element of game theory in the economics of decarbonisation, as the actions of others influence one's optimal development strategy. If the world's major consumer markets go green, there are high risks for economies that remain carbon-intensive, regardless of their income status. In anticipation of new green trade regulations and sustainability standards, countries will have to shift their productive capabilities towards the export of green goods and services to retain access to the largest consumer markets. The European Union's (EU) recent Carbon Border Adjustment Mechanism (CBAM) is a case in point, as it is estimated to cause losses of up to $31 billion across the African continent (Aggad and Luke, 2023).

(4) Delaying greening can hinder a country's ability to seize market and investment opportunities that decarbonisation provides, thereby missing out on thegaining first-mover advantage in some strategic industries.

If we understand development as being about opening pathways to prosperity rather than locking in non-viable growth, which is the view that this Element takes, then early greening (including in developing and fossil-fuel-dependent economies) can help bring about a range of benefits and open up new entry doors for industrialisation by gaining a foothold in the markets of the future (Pegels and Altenburg, 2020). As best phrased by Carlota Perez (2016), 'increasingly, the greatest window of opportunity of the present day is the possibility of overcoming the contextual legacy of the previous paradigm; in this case, the environmental degradation and resource scarcity brought about by the age of oil and mass production.' And in many ways, the global green transformation also provides a new direction for techno-economic development (Lema and Perez, 2024). The synergies between economic development and sustainability are further explained in what follows, with specific reference to the green reconfiguration of industrialisation.

Industrialisation is Dead. Long Live (Green) Industrialisation?

The role that industrialisation can play in the context of ecological sustainability is often overlooked and misunderstood. Both neoclassical and degrowth economics (or at least part of it) can be accused of a methodological fixation on consumption, with much less attention devoted to what sustainability entails in terms of the transformation of productive structures. Humanity does have a consumption problem, but the challenge of ecological sustainability goes beyond consuming less or differently, as it also involves an ancillary shift towards low-carbon manufacturing, given the important potential that new technologies and manufacturing transitions have in drastically reducing the material and energy content of consumption patterns (Anzolin and Lebdioui, 2021; Okereke et al. 2019; Perez, 2016). Nonetheless, industrialisation as we know it has to change. Historically, industrialisation has had a pernicious ecological impact (industry currently accounts for 30 per cent of GHG emissions globally). However, we must not throw the baby with the bathwater: climate-compatible industrialisation model is possible but needs to be based on new principles of resource efficiency and durability. In the following, I describe three main channels in which sustainability and industrialisation goals mutually reinforce each other.

(1) Seizing 'green windows of opportunity' for industrialisation: It is increasingly evident that the large-scale deployment of low-carbon technologies opens a new wave of opportunity for industrialisation, the so-called 'green window of opportunity' (GWO) (Lema et al., 2020). Though there are blocked routes to standard industrialisation given intense competition (Morris et al., 2012), nations can still be early movers in 'industries without smokestacks' (Newfarmer et al., 2019), which hold considerable potential for jobs creation and technological innovation (see Section 4). Opportunities exist to industrialise not only by integrating key segments of low-carbon technology supply chains (e.g. the manufacturing of electric batteries) but also by taking advantage of abundant clean energy generation as feedstock to develop competitive energy-intensive services and manufacturing activities.

(2) Clean energy transitions as enablers of the Fourth Industrial Revolution (4IR): Energy transitions are a backbone pillar to sustain the 4IR, which is defined as the advent of 'cyber–physical systems' involving entirely new capabilities for industrial production. Whether it is digitalisation, automation, artificial intelligence, 3D printing, blockchains, the Internet of Things (IoT), or Big Data, the 4IR technologies are highly energy-intensive and can consequently generate a high carbon footprint. Estimates suggest that the energy demand of the Information and Communication Industry is already higher than the aviation sector (Freitag et al., 2021).[3] Given the already increasing calls by the international community to reduce the environmental impact of artificial intelligence systems and data infrastructures (Balsameda et al., 2022; UNESCO, 2022), the 4IR will have to go hand in hand with clean energy deployment and broader ecological sustainability. In that perspective,

---

[3] In 2007, computers, data centres, and networks already consumed about 10 per cent of the world's electricity (Gartner, 2007).

failure to ensure access to cheap, reliable, and clean energy sources in some nations may hinder their ability to uptake a state-of-the-art industrialisation strategy. In those contexts, the 4IR may not offer the anticipated 'leap' forward (Mazibuko-Makena and Kraemer-Mbula, 2021).

(3) Value addition through environmental upgrading and circular economy: The classic understanding of economic upgrading has been linked to improvements in the ability of firms to move into more profitable and/or technologically sophisticated economic niches (Gereffi, 2019). However, over the past decade, the environmental dimensions of value addition have started gaining attention, which has led to the concept of *environmental upgrading*, whereby value is created by adopting environmental measures in value chains (De Marchi, Di Maria, and Micelli 2013; Ponte, 2019; Khan et al., 2020).

Environmental upgrading can generate process, product, as well as inter-sectoral upgrading. *Process upgrading* occurs by increasing production efficiency either through better organization of internal processes or the use of superior technology (Humphrey and Schmitz, 2000). Circular economy approaches, which involve careful management of material flows and aim to decouple economic growth from the consumption of finite resources by reducing and reinserting waste into production processes (Ellen MacArthur Foundation, 2015), are particularly relevant for *process upgrading* as they can entail considerable net material cost savings for manufacturing sectors. Increasing resource efficiency can lead to higher cost competitiveness, as firms require less inputs to produce the same amount of outputs.[4]

Sustainability measures can also generate *intersectoral upgrading* (also known as chain upgrading), which denotes the entry of a firm into a completely new value chain using capabilities acquired through the production of another good. In contrast to linear production systems, where growing trade in non-valuable scrap and waste exacerbates environmental damage and leads to the dumping of waste from developed to developing regions which often have weaker regulations (as illustrated by the case of dumping of used apparel in Chile, Al Jazeera, 2021), circular production systems present an opportunity to use these materials as valuable input for production processes in other industries (Ellen MacArthur Foundation, 2015). Indeed, synergies exist in terms of demand and supply of waste material and its re-use across different supply chains across countries, which can help improve productivity and provide new

---

[4] This process has also been termed 'eco-efficiency' which essentially implies combining environmental and economic performances to produce more goods and services while using fewer resources and creating less waste

opportunities for firms to enter new value chains. For instance, in Uruguay, dairy farmers who began to reuse organic waste from their cows to produce biofuels were able to generate as much as 40% additional revenues from biofuel production, besides milk production.[5]

Lastly, sustainability measures can help achieve *product upgrading*, that is increasing the competitiveness and value of products by increasing their durability and/or lowering their environmental impact. To remain competitive in the context of sustainability trends and increasing consumer preference for products that have a lower carbon and material footprint, firms can capture market premiums through product differentiation for goods and services whose eco-friendliness either lies in their production (e.g. clothes made out of recycled material) or their consumption (e.g. re-usable cups, electricity-saving gadgets, or durable/easily repairable products). Beyond the expectations of direct monetary returns (as eco-friendly options tend to have a higher price tag than regular products), firms may also adopt sustainability measures to reap reputational value. Recent studies even show that a firm's reputation for being committed to sustainability is an intangible resource that can increase the value of a firm's expected cash flows. (Lourenço et al., 2014)

For all the aforementioned reasons, we must go beyond an unproductive confrontation between the sustainability and the industrialisation agenda. However, not all countries are equally well-positioned to benefit from green industrialisation opportunities, and some have already taken a head start.

Conforming or Defying Comparative Advantage to Acquire Green Productive Capabilities?

Why is China better than everyone else at producing solar panels? Why is Denmark so good at producing wind turbines? Why is Austria one of the largest exporters of hydropower equipment? Can the performance of these countries be solely explained by the idea that they have a comparative advantage in producing those goods?

For understanding how countries acquire new productive capabilities required for green industrialisation, it is worth going back to the longstanding debate on whether state interventions should conform or defy comparative advantage (see Lin and Chang, 2009). The concept of comparative advantage, one of the core concepts of economics invented by Ricardo over 200 years ago, stipulates that nations can gain an international trade advantage when they focus on producing goods that produce the lowest opportunity costs as compared to

---

[5] Personal communication with Manuel Albaladejo, UN official in Uruguay.

other nations. However, many countries have industrialised successfully by developing capabilities and learning by doing in sectors in which they did not have comparative advantage (Chang, 2006). In that sense, static interpretations of the concept of comparative advantage tend to be path-dependent upon established capabilities, thereby consolidating the status quo as they have been mostly unfavourable to industrial development in poor countries where pre-existing capabilities often lack and have tended to condemn them to export unprocessed natural resources that they dispose of (which can be quite problematic in the context of climate change as explained in Section 2).[6]

As shown in Figure 1, most countries with a revealed comparative advantage in low-carbon technology products and environmental goods tend to be already industrialised, mostly high-income nations (especially in East Asia, the EU, and the USA). If the transition to a low-carbon economy enables high green industrialised prospects for already industrialised nations while renewing the limited role of most developing countries as sources of raw materials, the status quo is

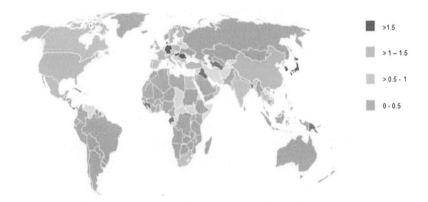

Figure 1 Revealed comparative advantage in low-carbon technology products and environmental goods (2019–2021)[7]

Source: Elaboration based on the IMF climate dataset

---

[6] For instance, emphasising principles of comparative advantage, several neoclassical economists wrote studies in the 1970s discouraging the Malaysian government to purse processing and industrialisation of domestic natural resources, which eventually become globally competitive thanks to infant industry protection (see Lebdioui, 2020).

[7] Though they overlap, environmental goods and low-carbon technology goods refer to slightly different things. Environmental goods include both goods connected to environmental protection (e.g. catalytic converters for vehicles, and compost containers) and goods that are adapted to be more environmentally friendly (e.g. biofuels, mercury-free batteries, and electric cars). Meanwhile, low-carbon technology products are those enabling decarbonisation by producing less pollution than their traditional counterparts, and include wind turbines, solar panels, and carbon capture equipment.

likely to increase economic disparities within countries, which casts doubts on the central promise of the UN sustainable development goals to leave no one behind. Some distinctions must also be drawn between 'developing countries', which, as a category, lump together countries facing very different situations, ranging from China, Malaysia, and Mexico, which have developed green industrial capabilities, to low-income commodity-based nations such as Suriname, Togo, and Papua New Guinea. For this reason, this Element will often refer to industrialised and latecomers, or specially refer to commodity-dependent developing nations in the context of acute exposure to climate risks (see Section 2).

Rather than accepting that countries have gotten where they are by exploiting their existing comparative advantages, the key question we should ask is *how* they have developed new productive capabilities and acquired new comparative advantages. In that sense, dynamic approaches to comparative advantage (which feature more prominently in the structuralist, neo-Schumpeterian, developmentalist, and institutionalist schools of economics) feature a wider scope for the role of the state, responsible for shaping productive transformation away from 'low-quality activities' towards 'high-quality activities' that are characterised by economies of scale, technological upgrading, high productivity and wages (see Chang, 2003; Cimoli et al., 2009; Mazzucato, 2016; Nurske, 1961; Perez, 2010, 2016; Salazar-Xirinachs, 1993). As further explored in Section 4, such an approach is better suited to explain the role that state interventions have had in stimulating the acquisition of green productive capabilities in several developed and developing countries (Altenburg and Rodrik, 2017; Anzolin and Lebdioui, 2021; Lema and Lema, 2012; Mazzucato, 2015, Newfarmer et al., 2019, Pegels, 2014).

The rationale for comparative advantage-defying policies is even stronger in the case of developing nations, where substantial market imperfections are more likely to persist in hindering industrial activities, technology transfer, adoption, innovation, and learning-by-doing. Rather than implying that those conditions make industrial policies too risky (which is the common critique of industrial policy in developing countries), they justify why government interventions are needed in the first place to efficiently reorient scarce capital towards priority areas with high spillover effects. This, of course, requires appropriate governance mechanisms and institutional structures to avoid inefficiencies, distortions, elite capture, and corruption. However, such governance mechanisms can be built. Our focus should therefore turn to how to improve the quality of government interventions to acquire new areas of comparative advantage, rather than accepting the status quo as a fait accompli. It is through such an approach that this Element will explain the dynamic process of green industrial development and its implications for developing nations.

Varieties of Green Economic Transformation and the Slippery Slope of Isomorphic Mimicry: It's Not Just about Producing Low-Carbon Tech

When it comes to green economic transformation, isomorphic mimicry must be treated with great caution.[8] In biology, isomorphic mimicry refers to how different organisms evolve to look similar without actually being related, in order to gain an evolutionary advantage. In public policy, it refers to the tendency of governments to mimic other governments' successes, replicating processes, systems, and strategies, and often ends in 'successful failure' (Andrews et al., 2017).

There is a growing tendency to mimic other governments' green industrial-isation strategies. For instance, over twenty governments have implemented local content requirements in renewable energy sectors, following China's successful experience with that instrument, but none of them reached a similar outcome (see Section 4). While it can be useful to learn and emulate others, it must be stressed that green economic transformation can take various forms, whose suitability depends on local contexts and capabilities, but this is also due to the multifaceted nature of our sustainability challenge. We tend to equate sustainability with decarbonisation, but there are other critical aspects of sustainability that also have implications for economic transformation, such as dematerialisation given the threat posed by material pollution to nature and human health, the sustainable exploitation of renewable resources such as fishing, forests, and water, as well as the alarming rate of biodiversity loss.

In practice, green economic transformation can also take the form of four distinct – albeit not mutually exclusive – processes (Chang, Lebdioui, and Albertone, 2024). The first process (which is what we often have in mind when referring to green industrialisation) consists in the production of 'green' technologies (often those at the heart of the transformation of the global energy matrix) that replace conventional technologies.

The second process consists in improving resource efficiency (both energy and material) in existing production, which can be achieved by:

(1) Adopting cleaner production processes (i.e. by shifting to clean energy sources to power industrial operations for green steel production)
(2) Improving the durability of products and allowing for easier repair, reuse, and longer product lifespan (e.g. durable and repairable consumer electronics)
(3) Reorganising production processes in a way that reduces resource needs (adoption of circular economy principles)

---

[8] Thank you Peter Robinson for bringing this concept to my attention.

The third one consists in mitigating the negative externalities from industrial activities that are already taking place. This process involves industries related to pollution control, geoengineering, and resource management (such as industrial air filters, carbon capture, utilisation and storage technology, and equipment for wastewater treatment).

The fourth process (which we can dub the Khaby process[9]) consists in the production of 'old' environmentally friendly goods that may not involve complex technology but that can nonetheless offer obvious ecological and economic spillovers (such as bicycles, organic agriculture, or multi-use products to replace single-use plastics). This process of sustainable industrialisation is often neglected, as it may not capture the attention of techno-optimists, but holds considerable value for sustainable industrialisation (see the discussion on the exclusion of bicycles as part of the environmental goods agreements in Section 6).

In sum, green economic transformation is a multi-dimensional process that extends beyond low-carbon technology production. The optimal path to green economic transformation will also vary significantly across different countries and regions based on their own circumstances, possibilities, and constraints. Pursuing deforestation in biodiverse areas or arable lands to make room for solar panel factories goes against principles of sustainable development, and other pathways to green economic transformation exist (as further explained in Section 5).

Outline of this Element

This Element is structured as follows. Section 2 explains the disproportionate economic impact that climate change and global decarbonisation will have on developing countries, before drawing theoretical and practical implications on how to rethink the concept of climate resilience and its implications for productive economic transformation.

Section 3 evidences the uneven industrial geography of decarbonisation by showing how most of the jobs, trade, innovation, and value derived from low-carbon technologies have been captured in a handful of industrialised economies. This has considerable implications for the 'leaving no one behind' agenda, as countries that are the most exposed economically to climate and transition risks are not those poised to benefit from emerging green industrial opportunities.

---

[9] In reference to the social media personality known for his videos in which he silently mocks overly complicated 'life hack' videos by performing the same task in a simple way.

This brings us to the role of governments in Section 4, which emphasises the role of green industrial policy, its factors of success, its different 'styles' (whether escorting or disciplining), and its political economy constraints and institutional requirements. This section explains that although there are some universal lessons that can be applied, green industrial policy needs to be adapted to local circumstances, and its objectives will differ across countries.

Furthermore, if all countries aim to industrialise simultaneously by manufacturing low-carbon technology, global demand may not support such a rapid expansion of production, leading to reduced overall growth and development. This is why, to better illustrate the varieties of green economic transformation pathways that exist beyond traditional manufacturing-led industrialisation, Section 5 examines different contexts and their implications for development strategies (including climate-smart agriculture in regions dominated by arable land, value-added nature-based services in biodiverse regions, fossil-fuel producers, and small nations/nations with a limited domestic market size).

Section 6 explores some of the international hurdles to green economic transformation, such as the rise of green protectionism in major markets, double sustainability standards, and the broken climate financing pledges, which weaken the ability of developing nations to promote their own green economic transformations. I argue that rich nations are effectively 'kicking away the *green* ladder' before discussing recent initiatives to reclaim policy space for green industrial policy.

Section 7 provides concluding remarks and identifies key trends that may influence the future of research at the intersection of development economics and ecology.

2 Rethinking Resilience to Climate and Transition Risks and the Role of Productive Diversification

> People are largely ignorant of the interests of the human species.
> — Ibn Khaldun (fourteenth century)

To date, most of the discourse around climate action has focused on addressing the symptoms rather than the root causes that make developing countries particularly vulnerable economically to climate and transition risks. Going beyond the unhelpful dichotomy between climate adaptation and climate mitigation, we need a better understanding of what climate-*resilient* economic development looks like. This section highlights the critical role of productive diversification towards that end.

How Climate Affects Trade and Financial Stability

Across the globe, precipitation patterns are shifting, temperatures are rising, and some areas are experiencing changes in the frequency and severity of weather extremes such as floods and droughts. However, not all areas are affected equally by the economic effects of climate change, and developing regions are particularly disadvantaged. African nations already suffered economic losses of approximately USD 38 billion because of climate change effects in 2020 alone (World Meteorological Organization, 2021a). In Latin America, it is estimated that climate change-induced damages could cost as much as USD 100 billion annually by 2050 (Vergara et al., 2013).

One of the reasons why climate change is likely to disproportionately impact developing countries lies in their higher reliance on the exports of commodities that are sensitive to climatic conditions. Fluctuations in precipitation and temperature threaten the long-term productivity of several agricultural goods that many (mostly developing) countries depend on as a source of revenue, jobs, and exports (see Figure 2). To note just a few obvious examples, climate change may pose a serious risk to salmon farming in Chile, coffee bean production in Vietnam and Colombia, cacao production in Cote d'Ivoire and Ecuador, or wine production in South Africa (see Conway, 2020; Macías Barberán et al., 2019; Soto et al., 2019). The increased frequency of extreme meteorological events has already led to devastating effects on tradable sectors such as agriculture and nature-based tourism in many parts of the world.[10] For instance, in the Caribbean, the hurricane season resulted in an estimated loss of more than 800,000 visitors, which would have generated USD 740 million for the region and supported about 11,000 jobs in 2017 (Saget et al., 2020). In Guatemala, drought conditions throughout 2020 led to the destruction of 80 per cent of maize grown in the highlands (World Meteorological Organization, 2021b).

Economic vulnerabilities to climate change also pose risks to countries' ability to borrow capital. Developing countries already suffer from difficult financing conditions, with an average interest cost on external borrowing three times higher than that of developed countries.[11] Such excessive interest rates often prevent poorer countries from accumulating public savings (least developed countries (LDCs) dedicate an average of 14 per cent of their domestic revenue to interest payments, compared to only around 3.5 per cent in developed countries) (Volz and Aitken, 2022). This gap is worsening with climate

---

[10] This is particularly damaging in countries such as the Dominican Republic where tourism accounts for as much as 40 per cent of export earnings.

[11] Over the past decade, developed countries borrowed at an interest cost of an average of 1 per cent, while LDCs borrowed at rates over 5 per cent, with some countries paying over 10 per cent (Volz and Aitken, 2022).

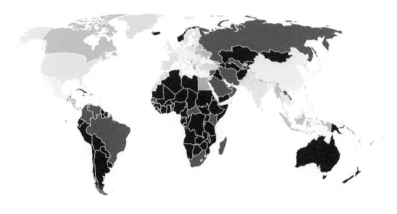

a)   as a percentage of allocated merchandise exports, 2019–2021

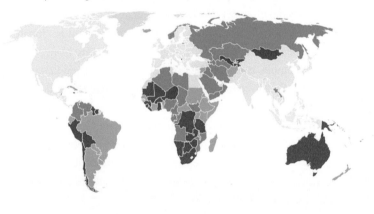

Dependence on energy products exports   Dependence on exports of agricultural products   Dependence on exports of minerals, ores and metals   Non-commodity-dependent country   Not available

b)   by dominant export product group, 2019–2021

Figure 2 Mapping commodity-dependent economies

Source: UNCTAD

change because developing countries are more exposed to environmental risks that are increasingly considered by financial rating agencies that give those countries lower credit ratings, which translates into even higher interest rates.[12] Soon, for every USD 10 paid in interest by developing countries, an additional

---

[12] Buhr et al. (2018) found that climate vulnerability has already raised the average cost of debt in a sample of developing countries by 117 basis points (which translates into USD 40 billion in additional interest payments over the past ten years on government debt alone).

dollar will be spent due to climate vulnerability (Buhr et al., 2018). To reduce the vulnerability of their financial systems to climate change, countries should not only adopt policies to reduce their exposure to environmental risks but also lobby for more stringent international action as many of those risks are beyond their national sphere of control.

Climate change knows no borders, and the adjustments that have to be made to avoid it are greater for some than for others (Stiglitz, 2015). Furthermore, the impact of climate change crosses not only national borders but also socio-economic ones. While most analyses of the economic impact of climate change (including this Element) consider regional or national economies through macroeconomic aggregates such as gross domestic product, or nationwide productive capabilities, such an approach can shadow some of the very important distributional impacts of climate change within countries (see Hallegatte and Rozenberg, 2017).[13] Climate risks exacerbate inequalities not only among countries but also within them.

The Impact of Global Decarbonisation: Transition Risks against the Right to Extract

Besides climatic risks, many countries are also exposed to transition risks, which refer to the financial and economic challenges that countries might face because of changes in policies, technology, market dynamics, and societal preferences aimed at addressing climate change (see Semieniuk et al., 2021 for a comprehensive review of the various drivers of low-carbon transitions risks for finance). One of the biggest transition risks derives from the drop in fossil-fuel demand. As the world draws closer to net-zero emissions, it is estimated that over 2.7 million jobs in fossil-fuel industries will be lost globally by 2030 (IEA, 2021). Although the use of petroleum in our societies will not completely disappear given the use of petroleum products for a wide range of non-energy products such as pharmaceuticals, cosmetics, and plastic goods, it can nonetheless be expected that the demand for petroleum will considerably decrease. For countries that consume a lot of fossil fuels, this implies an important shift in consumption and infrastructure towards low-carbon solutions, but for countries that depend on the exports of fossil fuels as a source of income (most of which are in the developing world, as shown in Figure 2), the prospects of global decarbonisation call for a more radical transformation of productive structures to avoid economic decline. In Africa, for instance, fossil

---

[13] Poor people can be heavily affected by climate change even when impacts on the rest of the population remain limited. In Nigeria, for instance, the most poor 20 per cent of people are 130 per cent more likely to be affected by a drought than the average Nigerian (Hallegatte and Rozenberg, 2017).

fuels currently represent around 40 per cent of total exports (sometimes reaching as much as 60 per cent in recent years).[14] In such contexts of fossil-fuel dependence and high carbon-intensity of productive structure, one major pre-occupation concern lies in asset stranding, which is the unexpected devaluation of assets from the balance sheets of economic agents (Caldecott, 2018; van der Ploeg and Rezai, 2020).

An important argument often put forward concerns the right to extract fossil fuels by communities that are not responsible and did not benefit from extraction in the past. If Africa were to use all its known reserves of natural gas, its share of global emissions would rise from a mere 3 to 3.5 per cent (Buhari, 2022). This is why indiscriminate calls for developing countries to keep fossil fuels in the ground can be misguided, especially considering that countries typically considered leaders in climate finance are extracting some of the most carbon-intensive petroleum in the world. On average, a barrel of Canadian oil is twice as carbon-intensive as a barrel of oil from Colombia and Ecuador, three times more carbon-intensive than a barrel of oil from Norway, and almost four times more carbon-intensive than a barrel of oil from Saudi Arabia![15] There is therefore a fair claim by global south nations to continue producing fossil fuels, while richer nations begin their phase-out.

However, the legitimate right to produce fossil fuel must be met with developmental pragmatism. Firstly, if current and future fossil fuel extraction is destined for exports, the profitability of such activity remains conditioned by the world demand for fossil fuels, which is influenced by the speed at which the global economy is decarbonised. Secondly, the rise of cross-border carbon taxes and sustainability standards may lower the competitiveness of activities produced with fossil-fuel-based energies. Lastly, even in developing countries, early greening, rather than relying on the extraction of fossil fuels, can help bring about co-benefits while gaining a foothold in the markets of the future, avoiding asset stranding (Pegels and Altenburg, 2020). As a result, even in countries that have not historically contributed to global GHG emissions, a forward-looking development strategy often implies favouring a green industrialisation pathway to avoid the risks of stranded assets and the risk of locking their economies onto energy-intensive pathways.

Meanwhile, we can expect the demand for the so-called critical minerals (that are essential inputs of low-carbon technologies) to significantly increase over

---

[14] Oil and coal face stronger headwinds of the global-energy transition, while the natural gas industry, given its lower CO2-to-energy content than other fossil fuels, may face favourable prospects in the medium term, depending on how much methane emissions can be reduced (Addison, 2018).

[15] Those calculations were conducted using figures from the Global Fossil Fuel Registry.

the next two decades, which causes great sources of optimism in countries that produce them. For instance, the Democratic Republic of Congo is one of the world's largest cobalt producers, Rwanda is the world's largest exporter of tantalum, and South Africa is the world's largest producer of platinum and manganese. In Latin America, Chile, Argentina, and Bolivia collectively hold most of the world's lithium reserves, while China dominates the production of rare earth. Today, these so-called 'critical minerals' represent a growing market.[16] However, risks also exist. The long-term outlook for these minerals is still dominated by uncertainty and risks of technological disruption, given the considerable R&D efforts globally to generate alternative technologies that rely on substitute materials (such as phosphate-based or hydrogen-based batteries to replace lithium-ion batteries, or substitutes to cobalt in electronics) (Manley et al., 2022). Furthermore, mined resources (and by extension their associated fiscal revenues) are non-renewable, at least from a producing nation perspective.[17] The economic decline of Nauru, a small island-country located in the Central Pacific, provides a cautionary tale: Nauru possessed one of the highest GDP per capita in the world (around $27,000) in the 1970s due to the rents generated by the extraction of its rich phosphate deposits (Trumbull, 1982). Nevertheless, a few decades later, the country was on the brink of economic collapse, as a result of the exhaustion of its phosphate deposits but also because phosphate extraction activities had damaged the island's arable land. In this context, one could argue that Nauru's phosphate reserves had a negative value considering its considerable opportunity costs and if we discount the lost agricultural value. Nauru's experience holds valuable lessons for governments today that are betting on the rising demand and value of their fossil fuels or critical minerals.

Productive Diversification as a Pathway to Climate Resilience

In light of the severe exposure to both climate and transition risks that some nations face, a radical shift is needed in terms of how we think about economic resilience in the twenty-first century. The global discourse remains dominated by an unhelpful dichotomy between climate adaptation and climate mitigation, with far less consideration for the core concept of *climate resilience*. Climate resilience has various definitions, but broadly entails the ability to anticipate,

---

[16] For instance, lithium, nickel, and cobalt are crucial to battery performance and longevity (International Energy Agency (2021b). An electric car contains twice as much copper than a car with a combustion engine (World Bank, 2017).

[17] One can argue that mined resources can be renewable as technology (to separate materials into their original components) conditions recycling costs and the ability to recover and reuse mined resources (such as cobalt or lithium in consumer electronics).

prepare for, and respond to hazardous events and trends related to climate, as well as to taking steps to better cope with – and avoid – new risks posed by climate change.[18] The absence of a coherent resilience paradigm (with shared definitions, problems, and methods) is a broader problem in economics and development studies as recently found in Park (2023). If the language of resilience is to advance collective prospects for development cooperation and climate action, then it will help to know precisely what we each are talking about (Park, 2023)).

In the context of climate change, the concept of resilience should cut across both climate mitigation and adaptation. Mitigation is a historical responsibility for rich industrialised nations that have disproportionately emitted GHGs, while climate adaptation measures often focus on the symptoms of climate change without necessarily addressing the structural roots that make some communities vulnerable to climate change in the first place. A more sustainable response to the climate crisis would emphasise policy and financial support for productive diversification, climate-resilient crop production, and early integration in low-carbon technology value chains as key enablers of the development of resilient and dynamic economies. For all the reasons mentioned in this section, diversi-fication strategies should be closely linked to a green structural transformation towards more sustainable production models in the long run to reduce the productive vulnerability to climate change and transition risks in resource-dependent countries. A wide range of new opportunities for green industrialisa-tion exist. However, as the next section shows, those are mostly seized by a handful of industrialised economies, rather than countries that are the most exposed to climate and transition risks.

3 Industrial Opportunities Arising Out of Low-Carbon Transitions: Who Benefits?

> Cui bono? (Who benefits?)
> — Marcus Tullius Cicero, Roman statesman and orator

The Socio-Economic Benefits and Industrial Spillovers of Low-Carbon Transitions

The benefits of the low-carbon transition spread far beyond the environmental domain. This is embodied in the notion of *co-benefits*, which can shape public opinion by lowering trade-offs among the diverse set of societal goals, such as economic welfare and environmental sustainability (see Anadon et al., 2016; Sovacool et al., 2020). Beyond their effects on ecological sustainability, there

---

[18] See definitions by the IPCC, IADB, and the Center for Climate and Energy Solutions.

are three main ways in which low-carbon technologies support economic welfare, which is further discussed in the following.

Firstly, clean energy technologies can help reduce the energy access gap for communities suffering from energy poverty. In Africa, close to 600 million people were still without access to electricity in 2018 (IEA, IRENA, UNSD, World Bank and WHO, 2021). This situation reinforces socio-economic inequalities and impedes progress in widening access to basic health services, education, and modern machinery and technology (IRENA and AfDB, 2022). In Latin America, businesses suffer 2.8 electrical outages on average per month, and nearly 40 per cent of firms in the region have identified the power sector as a major constraint for developing its full potential (World Bank Enterprise Surveys, 2023). Power outages also tend to exacerbate inequalities, as low-income households tend to experience more blackouts and power surges than high-income households (Inter-American Development Bank, 2014).

Secondly, low-carbon technologies can have an important employment generation effect. For instance, investing in energy transition technologies creates close to three times more jobs than fossil fuels do per million dollars invested (Garrett-Peltier, 2017). Jobs in renewable energies have steadily increased over the past decade to reach 12.7 million in 2021 and could reach 38 million jobs by 2030 under the 1.5 °C scenario (IRENA, 2021). In Latin America, while it is estimated that 360,000 jobs in fossil-fuel extraction and fossil-fuel-based electricity generation will be lost by 2030, the transition to a green economy can create as many as 15 million net new jobs in the region, especially in solar and wind power (Saget et al., 2020).

Lastly, the expansion of low-carbon technologies also generates opportunities for industrial development, which matters because manufacturing is key to sustained economic development (Chang, 1994; Kaldor, 1967). As of 2021, Africa's average manufacturing value-added per capita (of about USD 207) was eight times lower than the world average (USD 1,683), because Africa's economic growth and employment generation have relied heavily on low-value-added sectors, such as raw commodity exports (Chang et al., 2016; ILO, 2019). To avoid replicating patterns of commodity dependence in the context of low-carbon transitions, developing countries can attempt to integrate higher value-added segments of low-carbon technology value chains (whether upstream or downstream), rather than sticking to the provision of raw materials and low value-added installation and maintenance activities. For instance, developing countries could take advantage of cheap and clean energy sources not only to decarbonise electricity generation but also as feedstock to attract investments in value-added energy-intensive services and manufacturing. However, as we will see in what follows, most of the industrial opportunities arising out of low-carbon transition have been captured by a handful of already industrialised economies, which evidences the reproduction of core/periphery relations and the contemporary relevance of the dependency theory (Kvangraven, 2021).

The Uneven Industrial Geography of Global Decarbonisation

The economic benefits of low-carbon transitions may be vast, but who is capturing those benefits? By analysing employment, innovation, and export data, this section provides evidence of the extent to which the industrial geography of global decarbonisation is highly concentrated and shows that the communities that are most vulnerable economically to climate change and transition risks are not those where green industrial activities are taking place.

Jobs

The employment landscape in the renewable energy sector is concentrated in a handful of countries. Over 42 per cent of renewable energy jobs are in China, followed by the EU, Brazil, the USA, and India, which altogether account for three-quarters of renewable energy jobs. Meanwhile, the entire African continent has only captured about 2.4 per cent of jobs created in the sector globally, as shown in Figure 3. In Latin America, excluding Brazil, less than 500,000 jobs have been created in the sector to date (IRENA, 2020).

Besides the *quantity* of jobs created, there is also the matter of the *quality* of job gains that arise from the energy transition, where we can observe further unevenness. Decent jobs, that is, with good wages and safe work conditions, are

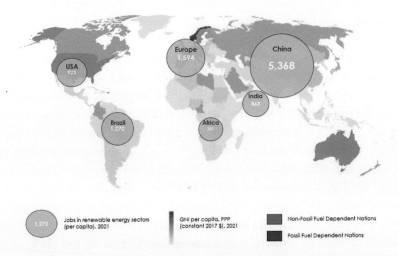

Figure 3 Global (uneven) distribution of jobs created in renewable energies
Source: Author's elaboration using data from the World Bank, IRENA, and UN Comtrade

necessary to ensure a just transition. However, most of the jobs created in Brazil, for instance, are in sugarcane plantations for biofuel production and in construction, operations, and maintenance activities, which tend to be temporary, low-paid, and low-skilled (Hochstetler, 2020).

Furthermore, as also shown in Figure 3, most of the job creation in renewable energy sectors has not occurred in low-income and/or fossil-fuel-dependent countries, where renewable energy jobs are arguably most needed to ensure a just transition. Looking ahead, compensating for the expected job losses in the fossil-fuel sector implies that more needs to be done in those countries to capture the potential job gains in the renewable energy industry. Policies aimed at facilitating the reallocation and retraining of fossil-fuel workers in other activities with quality job gains deserve particular attention (see Section 4).

Innovation

The capacity to innovate matters for making the most of the energy transition as an industrial opportunity and as a source of value quality job creation. Innovation and R&D play an essential role in the development, adaptation, and deployment of renewable energy technologies (Lema et al., 2015). Spillovers from low-carbon innovation are over 40 per cent greater than convention technologies in energy production and transportation sectors (Dechezlepretre et al., 2013). Here again, the low-carbon innovation landscape appears particularly concentrated. As shown in Figure 4, three-quarters of the

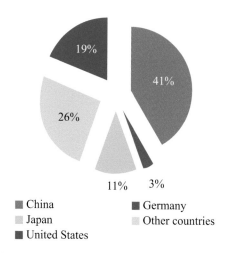

Figure 4 Distribution of patents filed in renewable energy technologies, by country, in 2014

Source: IRENA database

patents in renewable energy technologies originate from only four countries (which are also among the countries with the largest employment generation in renewable energy sectors, see Figure 2).

This is not to say that some developing countries have not achieved key successes around low-carbon innovation.[19] Latin American countries have spearheaded several R&D activities around renewables, including the development of short-term forecast tools for wind generation, hydrokinetic turbines for use with marine currents, smart mini-grids for electrification of isolated and rural communities, and biofuel production from microalgae (IRENA, 2015). Among those, one case worth highlighting is the R&D efforts that underpinned the successful development of biofuels in Brazil, which turned Brazil into the second-largest producer of liquid biofuels for transport in the world. Brazil's R&D capabilities around biofuels were supported by a range of governmental programmes (including the Network for Research and Technological Development on Biodiesel and the National Program of Production and Use of Biodiesel). Since 2006, Brazil's state-owned oil company, Petrobras, has also played a key role in supporting the production of – and R&D around – biofuels through its subsidiary, Petrobras Biocombustível, which led several R&D initiatives, mobilising nineteen public agricultural research centres (Nogueira and Capaz, 2013).[20]

However, notwithstanding some sporadic successes, patents filed in low-carbon technologies and R&D shares around low-carbon technologies remain extremely low in developing countries, mirroring a larger trend across sectors. This is not only due to limited public R&D efforts but also to an inability to attract private spending on R&D. For instance, more than half of the existing R&D expenditure is financed through public funds in Latin America, where the share in Europe, the USA, and Canada tends to be lower than 35 per cent. In Argentina, Ecuador, Cuba, and Costa Rica, the share of public funding in R&D exceeds 70 per cent (IRENA, 2015).

Export markets

It is a well-accepted fact among development economists that the ability to export is a critical feature of economic development. In the context of global

---

[19] For instance. Algeria had shown pioneering efforts in solar energy R&D, with the establishment of the Solar Energy Institute as early as 1962 (now called the CDER). However, success and commercialisation has been limited due to the lack of funding, unstable domestic demand, few incentives for competitiveness and productivity gains, and a failure to keep up with the growing automation of cell manufacturing.

[20] Ethanol production generates approximately thirty-two times more jobs per unit of energy produced compared to the petroleum sector (Nogueira and Capaz, 2013).

decarbonisation, the exports of carbon-intensive products will face increasing constraints, while considerable market opportunities arise for low-carbon technologies and environmental goods.

Similarly, to the job and innovation landscapes, the trade of low-carbon technologies is highly concentrated. Three countries (China, Germany, and the USA) account for almost half of all low-carbon technology exports (Figure 5). China's performance has been spectacular in that regard. Since 2000, China has increased its low-carbon technology exports tenfold and positioned itself as the uncontested exporter of low-carbon technologies (see Figure 6). As the next section will show, this was in large part due to the use of green industrial policies.

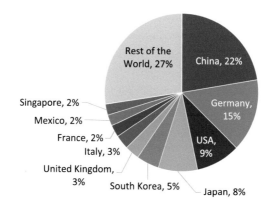

Figure 5 Export market shares of low-carbon technology products (average 2019–2021)

Source: Author's elaboration based on data provided by the IMF climate dataset

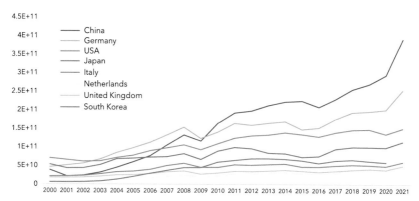

Figure 6 China's ascension in terms of environmental goods exports, 2000–2021

Source: Author's elaboration based on data provided by the IMF climate dataset

As shown in Figure 7, China's dominance spans different low-carbon technologies, such as solar cells, electric batteries, and hydropower equipment, where it holds 41 per cent, 30 per cent, and 19 per cent of global export market shares, respectively (see Figure 8). Meanwhile, Denmark and Germany are the two leading wind equipment exporters. Together with the Netherlands and Spain, they accounted for more than three-quarters of global exports in 2020. In the biofuels sector, the USA is the leading exporter (24.1 per cent), followed by the Netherlands (13.2 per cent) and Brazil (11.8 per cent).

The Reproduction of Technological and Trade Dependencies in the Hydrogen Sector

In recent years, hydrogen has received a surge in attention. An industrial gas used widely for more than a century, hydrogen has been historically produced using fossil-fuel-based energies. However, low-emission hydrogen can also be produced using renewable energies. Although it is still an emerging technology that bears risks and uncertainty, the so-called 'green' hydrogen is increasingly considered a critical enabler of global decarbonisation due to its versatility as an energy carrier and capacity to be used as a form of energy storage, thereby making energy systems more flexible and resilient. It also represents an interesting opportunity for developing countries: according to various studies, the areas where green hydrogen production costs could be the lowest (below USD 1.5/kg) are in Latin America (Northern Chile, Brazil, and Northern Mexico specifically), the Middle East and North Africa, as well as Southern Africa (see IEA, PWC, and McKinsey estimates).

However, there is a considerable risk that the hydrogen sector reproduces the patterns of commodity dependence that have prevailed with fossil fuels and mining. This is evidenced by the fact that most planned trade networks for hydrogen entail the export of hydrogen as a raw material from developing regions towards the EU and East Asia, where it can feed as an input into various industries and where value addition can take place (see IRENA, 2022). Furthermore, two-thirds of planned investments in announced hydrogen projects until 2030 (out of a total of USD 240 billion) are to take place in industrialised regions: Europe, North America, and East Asia. The picture becomes even more skewed in terms of the hydrogen investments that have already reached a final decision (about 10 per cent of them, representing about 22 billion USD), with over 85 per cent of those investments taking place in those regions (see Figure 8).

Breaking Out of Renewed Trade and Technological Dependencies

What can governments do to increase their country's share of global low-carbon technology investments, jobs, innovation, and exports? The global low-carbon

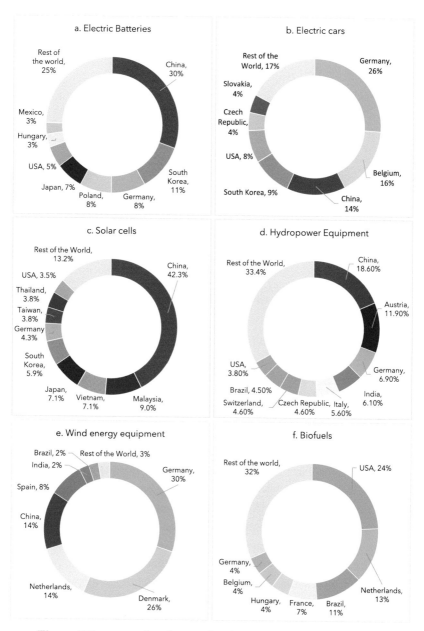

Figure 7 Export market shares of various low-carbon technologies by country in 2020

Source: Author's elaboration based on multiple sources, including OEC, UN Comtrade, IMF Climate data monitor and EurObserver'ER, and ITC databases

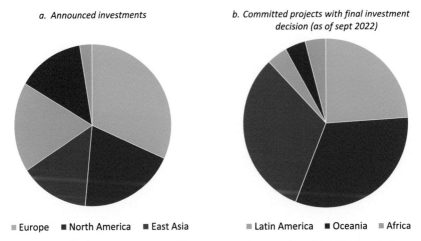

a. Announced investments   *b. Committed projects with final investment decision (as of sept 2022)*

■ Europe   ■ North America   ■ East Asia   ■ Latin America   ■ Oceania   ■ Africa

Figure 8 Distribution of planned investments in announced hydrogen projects until 2030

Source: Based on Hydrogen Council and McKinsey & Company (2022)

technology market is far from having reached saturation. It is estimated that by 2030, the market for low-carbon goods will be worth more than USD 1 trillion a year – an increase of seven to twelve times compared to today (Vieira, 2017).

As the global low-carbon economy increases, a radical policy shift is needed for developing countries to avoid being left – or even pushed – behind. Proactive public policies (and industrial policies in particular), which influence land, energy, capital, and labour costs are extremely important instruments in shaping the geography of low-carbon technology manufacturing supply chain (Hochstetler, 2020; Lebdioui, 2022a; US Department of Energy, 2022). Indeed, most countries that have become large exporters of low-carbon technologies are not necessarily the most endowed in terms of land and energy resources, nor do they have the lowest labour costs, but they have relied on proactive government interventions to develop the productive capabilities required to produce those goods. Understanding the policy tools underlying green economic transformation is the focus of the next section.

4 Governments as Referees and Head Coaches: The Political Economy of Green Industrial Policy

Free trade economists have to explain how free trade can explain the economic success of today's rich countries, when it simply had not been practised very much before they became rich.

— Ha-Joon Chang

Greening Development with More Markets . . . or More State Interventions?

Despite the widespread consensus among economists that climate change is the biggest market failure that the world has seen (see Stern, 2007), a key source of contention is the degree of government intervention required to fix climate change and transition towards a low-carbon economy.

On the one hand, some economists advocate for market-based adjustments (such as carbon taxes, carbon permits, and tradable rights) over interventionist policies. Market-based mechanisms aim to increase the cost of products that rely on carbon-intensive production processes by manipulating prices and, according to their advocates, these mechanisms should create the space for entrepreneurs to develop lower carbon alternatives (see Weitzman, 2007). According to Nobel laureate William Nordhaus (2007:29), 'raising the price of carbon is a necessary and sufficient step for tackling global warming. The rest is largely fluff.'

On the other hand, others have argued that carbon taxes and other market-based solutions are far from sufficient, putting forward a range of reasons:

(1) Carbon prices can be an ineffective signal for the uptake of unfamiliar technologies because of imperfect information. So far, carbon tax rates have been too low, do not internalise all externalities, and therefore do not correspond to the social cost of carbon, the estimation of which may vary considerably (Semieniuk and Yakovenko, 2020; Smith and Braathen, 2015).

(2) Even if the carbon price signal allows the market to adjust, pricing might not be sufficient to achieve on its own the scale and speed of decarbonisation required to stabilise global temperature at safe levels (Zenghelis, 2016).

(3) While it is often assumed that carbon taxes are progressive because richer people consume more CO2 on average (Gore, 2020; Knight et al., 2017), carbon market-based mechanisms can have a deeply regressive and discriminatory effect on low-income groups in practice, while paradoxically potentially allowing others to maintain their carbon-intensive consumption patterns and lifestyle by 'buying' their right to pollute. This is especially the case when alternatives to carbon-intensive services are too costly or inconvenient (for instance, the cost and length of train journeys are often higher than flights to the same destination). By making carbon-intensive services more expensive in an indiscriminate manner – rather than making greener alternatives cheaper and more attractive by subsidising them – carbon taxes can be quite regressive.[21]

---

[21] The *gilet jaunes* movement that has started in 2018 in France is a case in point, as the workers-led protests were the aftermath of rising fuel prices to support climate change (Atkin, 2018).

(4) Market-based mechanisms offer no guarantee that the socio-economic spillovers from green transitions will be localised where they are the most needed – that is, where communities are the most vulnerable to job losses due to decarbonisation, unemployment, and poor living conditions. Green transitions indeed provide an opportunity to diversify economies, but this requires appropriate policy interventions, especially considering the scale of investments that green activities need.[22]

A growing body of literature is therefore advocating for stronger government interventions in the context of the green transition. The remainder of this section reviews some of the key arguments put forward in favour of green industrial policy, its shortcomings, political economy constraints, and critical factors of success.

New Paradigm for Industrial Policy in the Context of Climate Change

An industrial policy can be broadly defined as the strategic effort by the state to encourage the structural transformation of an economy to enhance efficiency, productivity growth, and competitiveness (Chang, 2011). More specifically, it refers to 'any type of selective government intervention or policy that attempts to alter the structure of production in favour of sectors [or activities] that are expected to offer better prospects for economic growth in a way that would not occur in the absence of such intervention in the market equilibrium' (Pack and Saggi, 2006). Industrial policy can also be used to balance regional growth and assist workers to retrain or relocate, and consequently 'defuse the resistance to economic change likely to come from those who would be the hardest hit' (Reich, 1982), which holds particular relevance in the context of low-carbon transition (Lebdioui, 2022a).

From the 1980s until the early 2020s, industrial policy had lost popularity due to the ideological dominance of free market economics, a selective interpretation of failures in various regions (especially in Africa and Latin America), and the implementation of structural adjustment programmes, which led to the minimisation of the role of the state and premature deindustrialisation in many cases (Albaladejo, 2020). But the tide is turning: industrial policy has witnessed a revival in popularity around the world, based on an acknowledgment that they have been necessary ingredients of the acquisition of new comparative advantages in the past but also essential in seizing the so-called 'green windows of opportunities'.[23] Even in nations such as the United States where the term industrial policy has been taboo in recent decades, there is now

---

[22] Hallegatte et al. (2013); Lütkenhorst et al. (2014); Rodrik (2014); Mazzucato (2015, 2016).

[23] See Aiginger, 2015; Anzolin and Lebdioui, 2021; Cherif and Hasanov, 2019; Hallegatte et al., 2013; Lütkenhorst et al., 2014; Lema et al., 2020; Mazzucato 2016; Rodrik, 2014.

an explicit acknowledgement by the Biden administration of the need for an industrial policy to compete in low-carbon technologies. One could argue that industrial policy had never left (Mariana Mazzucato's work shows how the United States has proactively stimulated industrial development through state interventions and a vertical R&D policy), but the change in the narrative is important and reveals how the sustainability agenda is shaping the legitimacy of state interventions.[24]

Some of the key drivers for current comparative advantage, such as human, institutional, and technological capabilities, are policy-induced. Sector-neutral (also called horizontal) interventions to improve general education, infrastructure, and the business climate are important, but they rarely suffice to promote export diversification, which requires the use of (vertical) industrial policies (Cherif and Hasanov, 2019; Lebdioui, 2019, 2020). Historically, governments have had a key role in the acquisition of new comparative advantages by catalysing targeted human capital accumulation; solving collective action problems in knowledge creation through R&D support; manipulating market signals through price control mechanisms; providing specific public goods such as infrastructure investment; and crowding-in private capital in strategic areas through national development banking and public venture capitalism (Amsden, 1989; Lebdioui, 2019, 2020; Mazzucato, 2016; Rodrik, 2004; Wade, 1990).

In the context of green industrial policy, there are various instruments in the toolbox, both on the demand-side and supply-side (see Table 1). Those policies have been extensively used across the globe, but especially in the USA, China, the EU, and Brazil. China features one of the most remarkable cases of successful green industrial policy, enabling it to become the world's largest exporter of low-carbon technologies, which include solar cells, electric batteries, and wind energy equipment. Green industrial policy in China has comprised a comprehensive set of tools (including R&D support, the establishment of national-level innovation centres focused on clean technologies and local content requirements) with effective coordination of demand-side and supply-side policies (Lema and Ruby, 2006).

Another instance of a successful green industrial policy is offered in the case of Brazil, where over 1.2 million renewable energy jobs have been created.

---

[24] For instance, electric car manufacturers Solyndra and Tesla Motors received guaranteed loans from the US Department of Energy (of respectively USD 500 million and USD 465 million), and further benefited from federal tax credits for consumers buying electric car as well as fuel efficiency standards, which incentivised the larger market demand for electric vehicles (EVs), further boosting the productivity of EV producers through economies of scale (Mazzucato, 2013, 2016). More recently, industrial policy has made an explicit return as part of the Inflation Reduction Act, which aims to spur investment in green technology in the United States by devoting $369 billion in subsidies through grants, loans, and tax credits to public and private entities.

Table 1 The green industrial policy toolbox

Demand-side	Supply-side
• Fiscal incentives for low-carbon technology consumption	• Fiscal incentives for low-carbon technology production
• Public procurement	• Subsidised credit to firms (often through national development banks)
• Environmental regulation and penalties	• Public financing for R&D support
• Local content requirements (only effective in specific conditions)	• Public investment in related infrastructure
• Import constraints	• Green skills development programme
• Price control mechanisms	• Public provision of a clean electricity matrix to firms

The Brazilian National Development Bank has played a crucial role in financing the wind turbine manufacturing industry, providing loans and credit lines (at rates well below market levels) to incentivise value addition around renewable energy projects, especially for local wind turbine manufacturing, while imposing local content requirements (Hochstetler, 2020). The various local content requirements slowed the actual introduction of wind power until after 2009 but eventually contributed to a substantial national industry as they became 'the most effective guarantor of ongoing localised production of electricity components' (Hochstetler, 2020). Brazil has also established itself as a global leader in biofuel production, notably thanks to proactive R&D support and coordinated demand-side policies (Szklo et al., 2005). In other parts of the world, to date, the use of green industrial policies has been more limited and much less effective. Understanding how to adapt green industrial policymaking to the context of latecomers therefore deserves much more emphasis, which is the focus on the following subsections of this section.

Not All Green Industrial Policies Are Ecologically Sound or Good Policy

Most successful instances of green industrial policy are found in countries with a very large population size (such as China, the USA, Brazil) that could rely on demand-side policies to generate economies of scale. The challenge for countries with smaller domestic market sizes is that they face different challenges, and therefore replicating the same green industrial policy tools that work somewhere else might not be advisable (see Section 6). For instance, on the African continent, most green industrial policy tools implemented to date consist of local content requirements in solar and wind energy projects (especially in Algeria, Nigeria, and South Africa).[25] However, especially in countries with a small domestic market, local content requirements rarely work on their own, and their poor implementation can reduce the attractiveness of investments in renewables, or even worse, they can increase the levelised cost of energy (LCOE), thereby reducing the cost competitiveness of downstream industries. In fact, to date, only two out of seventeen countries globally (namely China and Spain) that implemented local content requirements (LCRs) in the solar and wind sector managed to develop export-oriented sectors. To stand a chance, different green industrial policy tools (especially local content requirements) must be integrated into a wider strategic vision of industrial development, adapted to the existing domestic capacity, and oriented towards long-term competitiveness.

Some so-called 'green' industrial policies may also generate more environmental damage without proper environmental appraisal capabilities. A narrow focus on carbon footprint reduction by extracting more resources from our planet may lose track of the broader view on sustainability and ecology and may generate higher material pollution, or even biodiversity loss (Chang, Lebdioui and Albertone, 2024). For instance, it would be unacceptable if scaling up mining to facilitate the low-carbon transition results in large environmental and social costs around mine sites and for local populations (Addison, 2018). Electric cars are the best example, given that their broadly ecological impact is not only determined by the source of energy in the electricity matrix their batteries are charged in but also their high material footprint given their very high consumption of lithium, copper, iron ore and other materials (see recent work contrasting lithium needs of electric cars and electric buses by Riofrancos et al., 2023). Another example is provided by green hydrogen production, which may be an emissions-free energy carrier, but can be quite 'unecological' in some areas given its water-intensive production, potentially drawing scare water resources away from agriculture and other sources of livelihoods for local populations. Therefore, for green industrial policies that truly aim to support the transition to a healthier planet, governments must also build strong environmental appraisal capabilities to integrate life-cycle analysis of environmental impact in their green industrial policy design. Social impact

---

[25] In South Africa, the Renewable Energy Independent Power Producer Procurement Programme was launched in 2011 to allow the state-owned utility Eskom to procure electricity from private producers through a competitive tendering process for which selection criteria include local content and local job creation (Eberhard and Naude, 2017).

appraisal capabilities can also help government assess the social benefits and cost analysis of their green industrial policies, paving the way for a socio-environmental approach that can be complemented by the use of conditionalities – standards and guardrails – that can be deployed through industrial policies to advance social welfare goals and the broader common good (Estevez, 2023; Mazzucato and Rodrik, 2023).

Aligning Industrial Policy within a Joined-Up Market-Shaping Policy Approach

The development of green industries has often been hindered by inconsistencies of objectives across various policy realms, as shown by a large body of literature on the importance of 'policy mixes', that is, the coherence, combination, and complementarity of various policy instruments to stimulate low-carbon transitions (e.g. Bahn-Walkowiak and Wilts, 2017; Palage et al., 2019; Rogge et al., 2017). Green Industrial policies are more likely to be effective if they are part of a joined-up policy approach and careful coordination with energy, environmental, skills, labour market, and fiscal policies (see Table 2).

The call for better coordination between related policies for green economic transformation should not stop at being an intellectual argument, as it also entails some changes in the organisational structure of governments. For instance, in contrast to conventional industrial policy, which has been historically led by a ministry of international trade and industry (the almighty MITI) in several countries, green economic transformations require coordination across a much larger variety of actors. The new set of institutional capabilities required for green economic transformation can include a coordinating body between the relevant ministries (finance, industry, trade, energy, environment, science and technology, education) as well as other entities, especially the central bank (Dikau and Volz, 2021), so that policies do not work at cross-purposes but instead amplify synergies.

As further explained in the following subsections, the value of a joined-up policy approach also derives from the need to address transversal challenges in the transition to a low-carbon economy, such as the social inclusion dimension of green industrial policy as well as the excessively high cost of capital for clean energy projects in developing countries.

Distributional Effects of Green Industrial Policy: 'Escorting' Versus Disciplining Approaches and Their Implications

How can we ensure that green economic transformations do not increase inequalities across income, gender, and ethnic lines within a country? Section 3 has focused on how decarbonisation stands to increase economic disparities between

Table 2 Multidimensional and overlapping policy tools for green economic transformation

	Industrial policy	Fiscal policy	Skills policy
Purpose	Promote the structural transformation of the economy in a way that promotes resilience to climate change and aligns with the market needs of a low-carbon global economy.	Increase public financing and patient capital for transformative green projects, notably through coordination between central banking and national development banking.	Support the acquisition of skills that are necessary to localising and creating green jobs, thereby improving readiness to seize economic opportunities arising from the green economy.
Challenges	Require considerable institutional capacity to implement, as well as monitoring and evaluation mechanisms to uphold performance requirements and avoid elite capture.	Fiscal constraints, particularly in developing countries facing significant debt servicing costs, may constrain the extent to which governments can employ fiscal policy to promote investments within the domestic economy.	Need to be coordinated with industrial and social policies to avoid skill mismatches, which can damage productivity; and ensure that skills development also targets marginalised groups to help reduce inequalities.

	Energy policy	Environmental policy	Labour market policy
Purpose	Provide incentives, support for, and attract investments in the development and deployment of low-carbon energy technologies that underpin some types of green economic transformations.	Besides aiming to improve environmental outcomes, environmental regulations (such as efficiency standards, or carbon taxes) can take the form of demand-side policies to help steer economic transformation towards specific activities and technologies.	Avoid potential labour misalignments across time, space, and educational abilities to ensure that workers can adapt and transfer from areas of decreasing employment to new industries, notably through the provision of upskilling services.
Challenges	Though they can encourage local value addition, energy policies and renewable energy tenders that are not well designed, or include unrealistic requirements in terms of local content, can lead to slowing down renewable energy expansion, thereby slowing down the process of downstream industrialisation.	If not coordinated within a broader economic and industrial strategy, environmental policies (such as the reduction of fossil-fuel subsidies) might generate additional costs to firms and consumers (and disproportionately affect lower-income groups) without helping foster local productive capabilities and productivity gains.	Can provide challenging in contexts where the skills gap is too high between labour needs in areas of decreasing and increasing employment; where workers are not willing to relocated; and where fiscal constraints prevent the payments of benefits or employment subsidies for workers affected by low-carbon transitions.

Source: Author's elaboration

nations, but the industrial policy agenda, without proper safeguards, can also increase economic disparities within countries.

Economic transformations can indeed, at times, exacerbate inequalities, as evidenced by the case of Costa Rica. Notwithstanding the positive impact of Costa Rica's export sophistication for poverty reduction (see Franzoni and Ancochea, 2013), it also led to wage disparities between skilled workers in the industrial clusters located in the centre of the country, and unskilled workers and those living in coastal areas that have not been able to benefit as much from the emerging high-tech manufacturing sectors (Ferreira et al., 2017). Such an experience forms the basis of valuable policy lessons for countries aiming to promote socially inclusive green industrialisation, especially regarding the need to recognise that green industrial opportunities are not neutral regarding domestic winners and losers, and the need to coordinate industrial policies with social, skills development and labour market policies to tackle skills gaps and mismatches[26] that hinder marginalised groups.

First, an inclusive green economic transformation implies that workers can adapt and transfer from areas of decreasing employment to other industries, notably by acquiring green skills, which are needed to adapt and develop products, services, and processes to support a sustainable and resource-efficient society. To be most effective, green skills development needs to be integrated into the wider training and skills development policy rather than being seen as additional or separate from other forms of skills development (IRENA, 2021). In conjunction with green skills development policies, labour market policies are also needed to avoid potential misalignments, such as: (i) temporal misalignments when job losses precede job gains at a larger scale (e.g. closure of a coal plant preceding new activities in renewable energy); (ii) spatial misalignments, when new jobs are emerging in communities or regions other than those that lose jobs; (iii) and educational misalignments (also called skill mismatches), when the skill levels or the occupations required under the energy transition were not developed or needed under the previous energy system (see IRENA, 2022). For instance, in Chile, even though replacing coal with renewable power would create between 2,000 and 8,000 net jobs by 2030, the communities where coal power plants are located (and where coal power represents 7.1 per cent of employment) will still be negatively affected because there are no guarantees that workers will be able to get the jobs created in renewable energy sectors (Vogt-Schilb and Feng, 2019). In those cases, labour market policies will be essential to reduce popular resistance to

---

[26] Skill mismatches can lead to considerable wage penalties, especially for overqualification, that eventually affect both job and life satisfaction (See Palmer, 2017).

low-carbon transition in communities depending on fossil-fuel extraction activities as a source of jobs.

Secondly, it must be recognised that some of the existing green industrial policies strategies leave ample opportunity for elite enrichment at the expense of workers. This is especially the case if industrial policies only consist in generous support and tax handouts for large corporations with little conditionality. The different approaches to green industrial policy based on their intended distributional impact and the interests they represent lead to a critical distinction between the developmental and the de-risking state, leading to 'escorting' versus 'disciplining' industrial policy. As governments aim to mobilise private finance for green development, Gabor (2021) has raised the alarm regarding the dominance of the 'de-risking' agenda, in which the role of the state is predominantly to 'escort' private capital towards green investments. She explains that the de-risking state orients private capital into achieving public policy priorities by tinkering with risk/ returns on private investments in sovereign bonds, currency, social infrastructure, and most recently, green industries, leading to a state–capital relationship where capital dominates (Gabor, 2021; 2023). The EU Green Deal and the US Inflation Reduction Act (IRA) are both examples of de-risking strategies to generate elite support, whereas the state-directed approach in the CHIPS Act disciplines private capital into national security priorities for semiconductor manufacturing (Gabor, 2023). Development by de-risking poses severe limitations as it is not embedded within an autonomous strategic vision of the state, thereby structurally weakening its ability to discipline private capital into pursuing green industrialisation while enabling the new green rules to be written by powerful investors and governments in the Global North (Gabor and Sylla, 2023).

In many ways, this stands in contrast to the *developmental* state and the ability of the state to conduct market-shaping and market-creating policies (Mazzucato, 2016; Perez, 2016). Drawing on the developmental state literature, we can draw valuable lessons on how to balance incentives and disciplinary measures (carrots and sticks) for industrial development from the East Asian miracle, which saw countries like South Korea, Taiwan, and Singapore rapidly transform into economic powerhouses. Because government support was contingent on performance, firms that failed to meet targets or lagged in productivity faced the withdrawal of state support or even penalties (Chang, 2006; Hauge, 2020). It is generally acknowledged that conditionalities are important to the design of industrial policies and that their absence could hamper success or even worse, leading to parasitic relationships (Amsden, 1989; Mazzucato, 2016; Studwell, 2013). This approach to industrial policy ensured competitiveness, deterred complacency, and consolidated the 'embedded autonomy' of the State (Evans, 1995)

In the context of today's green industrial policy, emphasising the dual role of the state in not just escorting but also disciplining private capital is therefore essential to ensuring that green economic transformations do not only serve private interests but also development and social inclusion objectives. The discussion around the de-risking agenda also has relevance in understanding the nature of the policy responses to reduce the high cost of capital for renewable energy projects in developing countries, as further discussed next.

External Financing Hurdles and Constraints for Green Industrial Policies

The High Cost of Capital for Renewable Energy Projects as a Major Obstacle

Some of the most important pathways to green economic transformation (e.g. the low-carbon production of goods and services) rely on the local availability of clean energy sources. However, quite paradoxically, despite significant labour, land, and construction cost advantages, developing countries must often pay more for renewable energy projects than in Europe and North America (see Figure 9). In Africa, for instance, the cost of capital for renewable energy projects is even higher than for fossil-fuel investments and implies that the continent may miss out on 35 per cent additional green electricity production under a 2 °C transition pathway (Ameli et al., 2021). This of course leads to distortions and lock-in into carbon-intensive economic pathways, while constraining the ability of low-income countries to seize some of the green windows of opportunities. The extent to which unequal access to financing can consolidate existing disparities in terms

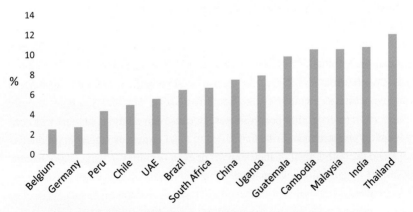

Figure 9 Weighted average cost of capital for solar PV projects
at 2017 interest rates

Source: Based on Steffen (2020)

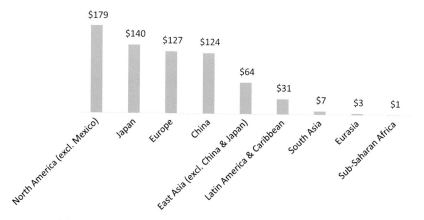

Figure 10 Renewable energy investment per capita in 2021
Source: Based on Wood Mackenzie, BNEF, and IRENA data

of energy access is well illustrated by the fact that in 2021, which had been a record year for global renewable energy investment (with around $420billion invested), renewable energy investment per capita was below $1 in sub-Saharan Africa, and over $100 in the USA, Canada, Japan, China, and the EU (see Figure 10). Indeed, while it is often assumed that renewable energy investments are first and foremost driven by natural conditions, it becomes evident that capital has not moved towards areas with the highest potential for renewable energy production, where they are the most needed (in terms of energy access gap), and that, in contrast to non-renewable resources, renewable energy investment is influenced by criteria that go beyond resource availability.[27]

There is an important debate on how to best lower the cost of capital for renewable energy projects in developing countries. Broadly speaking, the standard response has consisted of de-risking mechanisms, which can take two basic forms: measures that transfer risk ('financial de-risking') and measures that reduce risk ('policy de-risking'). Financial de-risking implies reducing the financial impact of a negative event by transferring large portions of the impact to other parties (often public institutions and taxpayers), while policy de-risking entails removing barriers in the investment environment and improving local institutions (Schimdt, 2014). As further explained in the following, each of those policy mechanisms presents pros and cons, different political economy implications, with different winners and losers.

---

[27] Indeed, Africa has an almost unlimited potential for solar capacity (10 TW), abundant hydro (350 GW), wind (110 GW), and geothermal energy sources (15 GW), with some estimates that Africa disposes of 39 per cent of the world's renewable energy potential, more than any other continent (IRENA, 2022).

De-risking Mechanisms: The Standard Response Advocated by Private Capital and the Alternatives

Financial de-risking entails transferring investment risks to public actors (such as development banks) to provide investors with a stable and predictable revenue stream. These instruments can include public guarantees, risk insurance, long-term contracts with guaranteed prices for renewable energy production through feed-in tariffs, power purchase agreements, and public equity co-investments. Another form of financial de-risking consists in incentives that can help lower the upfront costs of green projects, thereby making them more attractive to investors and more likely to get financed on better terms. Those include tax credits, low-interest loans, grants, and subsidies, for instance.

Though they seem to be easy fixes to the problem of the cost of capital for renewables, solutions that focus on financial de-risking tend to overly favour the private investors while transferring risks to public institutions, and by extension, taxpayers. Despite their tremendous benefits, renewable energy projects are technologically complex, prone to technological obsolescence, require several years of development, multiple-party negotiations, as well as rely on complementary investment projects. Therefore, they can often fail and are not risk-free. For instance, in South Africa, nearly half of the projects awarded under the launch of South Africa's renewable power purchase programme have failed (Mukherjee, 2023). By internalising too many of the risks in those projects, governments in developing countries essentially risk providing a handout to large investor groups, reaping little benefits in the long term.

This perspective also explains the downside of indexing renewable energy tariffs to a foreign currency (as suggested in Nelson and Shrimali, 2014) as a way of reducing the currency risks that hinder renewable energy financing in some countries. While this solution might reassure foreign investors, the effects it can have on domestic consumers can be dramatic in case of currency depreciation. A more viable alternative is to strengthen domestic financial markets (both at the private sector and public financing levels) to avoid currency risks and provide capital for renewable energy projects. To that end, national development banks (but also sovereign wealth funds for countries that have them) can play a catalytic role, with the provision of loans with below-market interest rates to promote green projects with high multipliers effects and spillovers.

Governments can also reduce the cost of capital for renewable energy projects by increasing their cost competitiveness through capacity-building and streamlining bureaucratic and regulatory processes. Those measures can generate considerable time and cost savings, which can help reduce the overall renewable energy development costs and make them more attractive to investors. Those policies will be quite effective in countries where the cost of capital is driven by a poor domestic policy environment. Nevertheless, in contexts where the costs of debt are high, those interventions will have limited impact without complementary efforts to reduce the cost of borrowing, which is the issue discussed next.

Lowering the Cost of External Borrowing: The Strengths and Limits of Green Bonds and Multilateral Development Banks

In some countries, the cost of capital for renewable energy projects is largely influenced by the costs of debt. For instance, in India, the cost and terms of debt can add an astounding 24–32 per cent to the cost of utility-scale wind and solar PV projects (Nelson and Shrimali, 2014). When domestic financing options are limited, there are various ways in which governments can secure foreign borrowing to finance renewable energy projects at a lower cost. For instance, governments can issue green bonds to raise capital for environmentally friendly projects at preferential rates. Since the issuance of the world's first climate bond in 2007, green bonds have gained popularity and their issuance has surpassed USD 1 trillion in 2021. In high-income countries, green bonds might offer little usefulness given that the projects they finance could have been financed with or without such mechanisms. But in developing countries, green bonds can make a big difference in terms of borrowing costs.[28] Many studies have investigated the notion of such a 'green premium' (or 'greenium'), but methodological heterogeneity among these studies has resulted in a lack of consensus over the size of such a premium. Some critics highlight that green bonds may suffer from higher transaction costs and lower liquidity compared to conventional bonds, potentially leading to higher borrowing costs for issuers and less attractive investment opportunities for investors (MacAskill et al., 2021).

Governments can also turn towards international cooperation institutions such as international development banks, regional development banks, and other institutions that can help mobilise additional financing for renewable energy projects and reduce the cost of capital.[29] However, the existing lending from multilateral development banks is far from meeting needs. Furthermore, while there are calls for the World Bank to increase its lending to developing countries and widen its scope to climate change-related projects, the World Bank's capital base is unlikely to expand. While in theory the World Bank's total capital base is $298 billion, in practice only 6 per cent of it (roughly $19.2 billion) has been paid

---

[28] In Latin America, the rapidly growing green bond market amounted to USD 21.6 billion between 2014 and 2020 (67 per cent of this amount has been issued by Chile and Brazil) (ECLAC, 2022).

[29] For instance, the EIB and Development Bank of Southern Africa recently launched a EUR400 million South Africa renewable energy investment initiative.

by donor countries and thus is available for lending (Usman, 2023). This is why international financial institutions (IFIs) are increasingly looking to turn towards the aforementioned financial de-risking agenda, in which their funds are used to provide guarantees to private investors in renewable energy projects in developing countries.

In sum, the effectiveness of different policy solutions is conditioned by the local context and the specific drivers of the high cost of capital, which differ from country to country. It must be stressed that a long-term solution requires tackling the considerable disparity in the cost of external borrowing, which is currently three times higher for developing countries than for developed countries, and which goes beyond renewable energy projects (Volz and Aitken, 2022).

Political Factors, Elite Bargains, and Institutional Constraints for Green Industrial Policy

The challenge of green economic transformation is not just economic, but first and foremost political. The economy operates within political and social structures that determine, in many ways, the ability to design and implement policies, and green industrial policies are no exception. Therefore, a key question we must ask is: why do some governments seek to build capabilities to foster green economic transformation while others do not? Is it due to a lack of policy awareness, or a perception that climate-related measures are not the responsibility of said country? Or is it the fact that greening development requires too much re-organisation of the so-called 'political settlements' (Khan, 2010)?

Several scholars have argued that a country's decisions around energy transitions and/or green industrial policies are the product of active coalition building and struggle among three key sets of actors defending their interests: state actors, business associations and firms (whether they are agro-business lobbies, fossil-fuel companies, industrialists, or the banking sector), and civil society groups (see Breetz et al., 2018; Hess, 2018; Hochstetler and Viola, 2012; Newell and Paterson, 2010). However, the interests of different groups are not static across time and space. Most successful experiences of economic development are not necessarily ones where the economic elites had been pro-developmental from the start, but instead reflected the state's ability to align different interests with the objectives of industrial policy, in line with the theory of embedded autonomy (Evans, 1995), which suggests that a developmental state needs to maintain a balance between autonomy from private interests and embeddedness in social coalitions with non-state actors. The aforementioned reasons therefore do not suffice in explaining why political and economic elites are at times able to strike new 'development bargains' (Dercon, 2022) to align their interests towards a green transformation agenda.

Recognising that states pursue green economic transformation within different political economies, entailing different interests and costs, Hochstetler (2020) introduces four major potential political economy drivers behind low-carbon transitions:

(1) Climate change mitigation (with diffuse collective interests in climate action and concentrated costs for fossil-fuel industries)
(2) Industrial policy (with concentrated benefits from firms in renewable energy supply chains and diffuse interests for growth and industrialisation)
(3) Increased energy distribution and access (with concentrated benefits for those without electricity)
(4) Concentrated benefits for hosting communities

While climate change mitigation objectives are often invoked by governments to justify their green industrial strategies, they often do not explain why governments choose to tackle low-carbon transitions in a particular way, favouring some low-carbon technologies and activities over others (e.g. why the EU has lobbied against the inclusion of bicycles in environmental goods negotiations, as further explained in Section 6). In the case of Brazil, Hochstetler (2020) explains that climate action motivations do not suffice to explain the scale up of wind over solar energy, despite the country's ideal conditions for the latter, and concludes that industrial policy and cost considerations are the political economies that best explain the different fates of wind and solar power in Brazil. More often than not, the political push for green economic transformations reflects geopolitical reasons and/or desire to seize industrial opportunities (e.g. China since the 2000s, and the EU and USA since 2020).

To better understand the various political economy dynamics that influence elite bargains, the buy-in for green industrial policy, and its broader success, the next paragraphs explore several factors, such as the time horizon of industrial policy planning, institutional layouts and constraints, as well as the influence of state–business relations.

Time Horizon for Industrial Policy Planning

A political vision will only take you so far if it is not sustained over time. The success of green industrial policies hinges on the stability of the political system and the long time horizon of policy planning, especially considering the long-term investments that green activities need. In democracies, ensuring policy continuity and long-term planning is a real challenge. If the political system allows for policy commitment across party colours (which is rare), it is easier for governments to implement long-term policies that favour green structural transformation. However, in the absence of such multi-partisan support, green economic policies can be easily overturned, leading to unstable energy and environmental politics that stunt the infant development of new industries. Recent history is filled with examples. In the United States, the Trump administration overturned several environmental commitments and measures adopted by the Obama administration, which reduced incentives towards greening industrial activities. In Brazil, the Bolsonaro administration incapacitated the government environmental agencies and scaled down public R&D support. Even in Sweden, which is normally considered a stable progressive country, the recent election of a right-wing government led to the reversal of several environmental commitments. The need to work across party lines is also well evidenced in the case of Chile, where, like many other Latin American nations, presidents are not allowed to seek consecutive re-election. This rule has important implications for the ability to engage in long-term industrial policymaking and led to the discontinuation of the industrial policy formulated by the first Bachelet administration (2006–2010) by the first Piñera government (2010–2014). The fear of 'renewed discontinuation' led to policy stagnation during the second Bachelet government (2014–2018), but also made the need to discuss industrial strategy across party lines more evident.

A useful case of long-term green policy vision is provided by China, which will be responsible for 60 per cent of new renewable capacity expected to become operational globally by 2028 (IEA, 2024). Starting almost from scratch in the early 2000s, it took less than a decade for China to become a superpower in the renewable energy industry. After its political leadership identified moving away from labour-intensive, resource-based, and energy-intensive industries as a strategic priority to circumvent the middle-income trap, green industrialisation has been a key part of the nation's development strategy, notably through the government's five-year plans (Lema and Ruby, 2007).

China's approach to green industrial policy offers valuable insights on the balancing of centralised long-term vision with localised short-term implementation. Most explanations of why China has been able to outcompete others in green industries emphasise its distinctive state-led model, involving active intervention by the central government regulators to create and protect the market (Chen and Lees, 2016; Hochstetler and Kostka, 2015;Shen and Xie, 2017; Xu et al., 2010). China's distinctive state-led model has led to a prevailing perception of 'authoritarian environmentalism', or 'centralised authoritarianism', characterised by top-down and non-participatory policy environment dominated by a powerful party-state (see Beeson, 2010; Gilley, 2012; Kostka and Mol, 2017; Liu et al., 2012). However, other scholars highlight a more nuanced and complex reality in the ground with a mixture of authoritarian and liberal features, in light of elements of decentralisation and space for local governments to act as representatives of local interests, rather than as mere agents of the central government (see Li, 2010; Lieberthal, 1992; Lo 2015). The inability of the central government to control local governments and firms in several instances reveals a relatively high degree of local industrial and energy policy space and flexibility despite the overt authoritarian rule (Lo, 2015). Far from a logic of top-down centralised authoritarianism, Shen and Xie (2017) also highlight the political struggles among central ministries, local officers, and non-state actors in the design of green industrial policies. China's case also features governance challenges, such as the high turnover of leading cadres at the local level which can hinder state-led green industrial policy, as suggested by Eaton and Kostka (2014). This frequent turnover, through intended primarily to facilitate implementation by reducing coordination problems, also entails significant downsides to local leaders who, by changing office every three to four years, might be incentivised to adopt the path of least resistance with short time solutions over long-term transformative ones. Local government intervention can also at times run against the directives from the central government, as has been the case for the excessive provision of bank loans at local levels, which resulted in huge amounts of short-term debt, which has turned into non-performing loans (Hochstetler and Kostka, 2015).

Despite these challenges and the fact that lessons may not be easily replicated in other institutional and political contexts, the key takeaway from China's experience is the importance of the balance between the central government's provision of long-term policy direction ('where to go') and the flexibility of local governments to design policies to deliver identified objectives ('how to get there'). In some ways, China's approach bears some resemblance to policymaking in federal systems (such as Malaysia) but also the EU, where a supranational body legislates on long-term targets while member states decide on the implementation strategies (though the EU has been far less successful at developing a regional green industrial policy, partly due to the resistance of some of the large member-states that seek to move faster on their own). The solutions that a country may find for integrating green industrial policy measures within a long-term vision vary based on the local institutional contexts, but what we can learn from different experiences is that they require active cooperation and coalition building with actors beyond the central government, such as opposition parties in some contexts or local governments in others.

We have established that having a long-term policy vision plan is necessary, but, as Mauritian economist Isabelle Ramdoo once told me, 'having too many visions can lead to hallucinations', especially when implementation capacity is lacking. The number of governments that have announced green economic transformation plans in recent years is too large to keep track of, but the number that possesses the institutional capacity to implement these visions is far smaller.

Development planning capabilities are critical for the careful design of green economic strategies that have the best chance of generating buy-in, reorienting the incentives of powerful stakeholders, and also ensuring long-term policy continuity. As explained by former Malaysian Prime Minister Mahathir Mohamad:

> Being methodical is the way to achieve success. [...] Method involves a series of pre-determined orderly steps and procedures, planned and laid out so as to achieve a certain objective. The country's development was being based on five-year plans, which enabled us to link the yearly budgets and give us a definite programme for five years. In addition, we had the long-term perspective of 10 years. The plans could not be segregated or kept apart from each other but had to be continuous so that each could coincide with the previous one. (2007:4)

Development planning and implementation require an effective bureaucracy (or plans to train public officials); necessary regulatory mechanisms (notably to enforce performance requirements); as well as financial and technical resources to implement, monitor, evaluate, and correct them if necessary. To avoid risks of elite capture and cronyism, which jeopardise the effectiveness of policy action and the state's 'embedded autonomy', industrial policy must also be subjected to legislative oversight and transparency around the criteria used to favour some sectors and activities over others.

Another major institutional constraint in green industrial policymaking relates to the recurrent conflicting interests between energy and industrial policymakers. For example, policies focused on fast energy deployment might neglect local industrial linkages around renewable energy projects, and policies focusing on developing an industrial base around renewables could compromise energy price competitiveness and accessibility. Traditionally, the primary role of energy regulators is to oversee domestic power generation, transmission, and distribution, while the oversight over the manufacturing of renewable energy technologies has been a less common direct responsibility of energy regulators, with this mandate falling under broader industrial policy and trade policy in most countries. However, China presents an interesting case where green industrial policy has been achieved through a unique institutional configuration that allows for coherent coordination between various ministries and public agencies.

Interestingly, China no longer has a dedicated Ministry of Energy in the same way that most other countries have, as it was disbanded (five years after its creation in 1988) precisely because the portfolio of that ministry overlapped with other ministries. Instead, its energy sector and green industrial policies are governed and regulated by multiple government bodies and agencies, with responsibilities distributed across these different entities. Instead the mandate of energy regulators in China (such as the National Energy Commission) extends beyond traditional power generation to include aspects crucial to industrial policy, such as manufacturing capacity, technology advancement, subsidy schemes, and overseas projects (Shen and Xie, 2017). The National Energy Commission was established in 2010 as an interdepartmental coordinating agency of the State Council, which is chaired by the premier and which coordinates the overall energy policies and includes twenty-three members from other agencies such as environment, finance, central bank, and the National Development and Reform Commission. Furthermore, all these 'central' ministries have local offices to support their regulatory and planning activities related to renewable energies and green manufacturing.

Far from a logic of isomorphic mimicry (see Section 1), the governance structure of China's energy and industrial policy has emerged rather organically to mitigate observed institutional conflicts over the past decade. In other countries, the decision-making processes and institutional capabilities for green industrial policy may differ significantly. For instance, many fossil-fuel producers have chosen to centralise decision-making ministries of energy, which can often lead to a disproportionate influence of the fossil-fuel incumbents over the clean energy/green industrial policy agenda. The Chinese model exemplifies a complex yet effective multi-ministry collaboration that has developed over time through institutional learning-by-doing, while other models might emphasise streamlined decision-making or integrated policy frameworks. The key lesson is that the institutional configurations must allow for policy coherence across different domains, but must evolve with the specific political, economic, and social contexts of each country to effectively drive green industrial policy. This is particularly important as countries are significantly more likely to introduce policies that require similar institutional capacity and policy know-how to policies they have previously introduced (Hallegatte et al., 2024). Realistically, green industrial policies are therefore also more likely to succeed if tailored to existing and organically evolving institutional capacity.

Differences in state–business relations contribute to explaining some of the observed green industrial policy trajectories across countries. For instance, while the USA, Brazil, and China have shared similar objectives in wind and solar power, China's context of state corporatist state–business relations explains why state interventions were more far-reaching than the other two countries, with the state coordinating with state-owned banks, offering large financial and investment incentives to state-owned or state-connected enterprises (Hochstetler and Kostka, 2015). By contrast, in Brazil, state support to promote local content around renewable energies have been shaped by a stronger preference for competitive auctions, stricter financing rules and public private partnerships (Hochstetler and Kostka, 2015; Hochstetler, 2020). The Brazilian political economy under Lula and his successor Dilma Rousseff has been broadly pro-business, focusing on public–private partnerships that worked well in the wind energy sector (Hochstetler, 2020). This 'soft' approach to green industrial policy favoured carrots over sticks, in contrast to China where the government has had more political room for manoeuvre to adopt a 'hard' approach.

The United States offers a hybrid case, with a mostly soft approach that includes some elements of a hard approach, as it heavily relies on subsidies (mostly through tax credits to corporations investing in green industries) combined with more protectionist local-content requirements. This can be largely explained by the domestic political context, the needed support from congress, and also the institutional ability of the federal government to implement policies through the Internal Revenue Service rather than through local governments, as was the case in the Chinese context.

In parallel to state–business relations, the political economy of green industrial policy is also largely shaped by public opinion, especially because this agenda can often entail short-term costs, while the benefits are only realised in the medium or long term.[30] Policymakers are often tempted to pursue populist and short-term measures to gain support from communities that depend on fossil fuels as a source of jobs (such as coal miners). From a political standpoint, preserving the status quo often appears as an easier route for re-election rather than embarking on the challenging and lengthy task of reskilling and implementing labour market policies to reintegrate workers from the fossil-fuel industry into more dynamic and sustainable segments of the economy.

---

[30] For example, the implementation of renewable energy sources incurs upfront costs but is ultimately more cost-effective and beneficial than relying on fossil fuels in the long run.

This is why a government's ability to communicate with the wider electorate and provide a compelling justification for green economic transformation is essential. For instance, in the USA, the measures pursued as part of the IRA and the CHIPS Act under the Biden administration have been framed as a national security necessity to counter the threat of China's technological dominance, rather than a climate-driven agenda. Such geopolitical framing enabled the bill to pass in congress and provided a justification for the programme. Paradoxically, but quite tellingly, despite Republican lawmakers' opposition to the climate agenda, Republican congressional districts hosted over 80 per cent of investments in large-scale clean energy pledged in the two years after the passage of the IRA.

There is a large degree of interinfluence between state–business relations and public opinion. Public opinion can push businesses to adopt a green agenda, but businesses can also influence (and even distort) public perceptions of climate change and sustainability. For instance, in the early 2000s, in order to weaken policy reforms targeting the role of oil companies in climate change, British Petroleum promoted and successfully popularised the term 'carbon footprint' to shift attention away from energy companies and towards the ecological impact of individuals' daily life activities and air travel (Kaufman, 2020). Against this backdrop, enabling a transparent multi-stakeholder dialogue around green industrial policy is critical to balance different interests and generate grassroots support for long-term transformative projects.

In sum, the promotion of green economic transformation models calls for proactive and coherent state interventions. But while the literature on green industrial policy is moving towards quantitative evaluations of the effectiveness of different instruments, the extent to which state–business dynamics and institutional arrangements shape the feasibility of those different instruments reveals the usefulness of bringing the study of comparative environmental politics and state–business relations to the core of qualitative explanations of green industrial policy. Each country's political, social and economic character-istics, such as the level of policy ambition, political leadership, the type and strength of domestic social coalitions, but also the starting composition of their productive structures, the size of the domestic market, and developmental needs deeply influence how policymakers choose to tackle this agenda, as well as its speed and scale. Researchers and policymakers may draw informative lessons from studying the experiences of developed economies (such as in the EU, Japan, South Korea, or the USA) and large developing economies (such as Brazil or China), but such experiences may not often be easily replicable.[31]

---

[31] Even in the case of India, Behuria (2020) argues that the country's position as a late, late industrialiser in the renewable energy sector, combined with prevailing domestic political

Countries attempting to develop green industrial capabilities therefore need to adapt their green industrial policies to their own economic, political, and social context. In that spirit, the next section therefore explores how different pathways to green economic transformation exist based on different country contexts and starting points.

5 No Green Silver Bullets: Various Pathways to Green Industrialisation beyond Manufacturing

> Those who doubt the potential dynamism of natural resources assume that there are truths about certain sectors that do not change over time.
>
> — Carlota Perez

Overview: Green Industrialisation Is Not All About Manufacturing

Countries across the globe find themselves at different starting points and circumstances in terms of productive capabilities, resource endowment and geography. Manufacturing low-carbon technologies is an important pathway to green economic transformation, but it is not feasible for every nation, not least due to a fallacy of composition. This fallacy posits that if all countries attempt to industrialise simultaneously, global demand may not support such a rapid expansion of production, leading to reduced overall growth and development. This is particularly the case when countries try to industrialise through the same industries and producing the same goods.

With the increasing scepticism of the universal suitability of manufacturing to serve as the driver for economic transformation, several scholars have argued that the modern services sector can instead act as an engine of structural transformation, given that it features many characteristics historically associated with manufacturing, such as tradability, knowledge and technology spillovers (Baldwin and Forslid, 2019; Gollin, 2018; Nayyar et al., 2018, 2021). The role of the service sector is also receiving increasing attention in the context of the transition to low-carbon economy. As the digital economy faces a sustainability challenge to reduce energy consumption and electronic waste of digital services, more opportunities for disruptive and skilled tradable green services are opening (including in terms of rental, repair and recycling services to guarantee product durability, see Perez, forthcoming). However, two points can be made. Firstly, Sen (2023) draws important distinction between business and non-business services, and shows that treating the service sector in

---

economy pressures, has made it extremely difficult to promote the manufacturing of solar panels and cells.

a monolithic manner does not take into account the differences that different types of services play in structural transformation. Secondly, the extent to which countries can leapfrog to value-added business services without first establishing a domestic manufacturing base can be questioned, as historically, value-added services are ancillary to existing manufacturing activities (Chang, 2006; Hauge, 2023).

This is why imported solutions do not often work, and nations should pursue development strategies that align with their contexts and priorities. A country's unique assets, such as its natural resources, biodiversity, agricultural potential, existing productive capabilities, and domestic market size, largely influence the available pathways to development. To better illustrate the different varieties of green economic transformation that exist beyond traditional manufacturing-led industrialisation, this section examines different contexts and their implications for development strategies (including climate-smart agriculture in regions dominated by arable land, value-added nature-based services in biodiverse regions, fossil-fuel producers, and small nations/nations with a limited domestic market size).

Climate-Smart Agriculture and the 'Industrialisation of Freshness'

In some countries, especially low-income ones, agriculture is the main pillar that sustains livelihoods but can also turn into the foundation for their future economic development. The role of agriculture for structural transformation has often been debated in the literature and is often misunderstood. On the one hand, a key insight from the structuralist school (and the Prebisch–Singer hypothesis in particular) is that the price of primary commodities relative to those of manufactured goods was bound to decline over time, dooming poor countries to poverty unless they industrialised (Prebisch, 1950; Singer, 1950). Indeed, the share of agriculture in a country's GDP and employment tends to decline with economic growth (Anderson, 1987). But on the other hand, several agricultural economists have argued that agriculture is a catalyst for economic development (Eicher and Staatz, 1998; Mellor, 1995; Schultz, 1968). In fact, as of 2019, the highest agricultural value-added per worker figures can be in industrialised countries such as the Netherlands, Canada, the USA, and Australia (World Bank, 2023).

These contrasting perspectives on the causal relationship between agriculture and the structural transformation of an economy are best explained by John Mellor (1966): 'The faster agriculture grows, the faster its relative size declines.' Mellor (1995) explained that the role that agriculture plays in the structural transformation of the economy is determined by several factors, including (i) how productivity is affected by technological change, (ii) how the increased income is spent, and (iii) what other sectors of the economy undergo expansion as a result of agricultural development and its linkages. Besides those three mechanisms, it can be argued that agriculture's continued relevance for long-term development is also determined by a country's ability to add value to its agricultural goods. Defining value-added agriculture is no easy task, as processing does not always equate value addition, and fresher products can be far more technologically sophisticated and generate higher returns than pro-cessed food (e.g. a fresh orange versus a carton of orange juice, or fresh fish versus canned fish). At the heart of this process is what Cramer and Sender (2019) call the industrialization of freshness', which matters for developing countries because of the considerable scope for productivity growth, export revenue growth and employment creation.

However, the aforementioned mechanisms are now heavily threatened by climate change, given that some types of crops are profoundly vulnerable to climate change (see Section 2) and the fact that current agricultural practices also exacerbate climate change (about one-third of GHG emissions are gener-ated from agriculture) (Ritchie, 2021). This is why climate-smart agricultural strategies emerge as an important agenda to help farmers protect their income and livelihoods while improving food security by enhancing the ability of agricultural systems to adapt and thrive under changing climatic conditions and reducing their environmental impact. Broadly speaking, we can under-stand climate-smart agriculture from a mitigation, an adaptation, and a productivity angle (Palombi and Sessa, 2013). The last two angles are those that hold the most relevance from a development perspective. From the adaptation side, climate-smart agriculture consists in enhancing the resili-ence of agricultural systems to climate-related risks. For instance, the diversi-fication towards climate-resilient crop varieties can help protect farmers' livelihoods from climate risks and ensure food security. From a productivity-side, climate-smart agriculture entails sustainable intensification, which con-sists in increasing agricultural productivity (through sustainable land and water management practices such as precision agriculture, integrated nutrient management, intercropping, as well as circular economy practices) while minimising negative environmental impacts (Campbell et al., 2014). For instance, studies have shown that Banana-coffee intercropping in East Africa helps reduce Arabica coffee's vulnerability to higher temperatures by provide shade, but also reduces incidence of coffee leaf rust, leading to an increase in plot revenue by more than 50 per cent (Van Asten et al., 2011). Improving resource reuse within agriculture production can also at times support product diversification and linkages towards other supply chains (intersectoral upgrading). For instance, improved cattle manure management by dairy farmers in Uruguay has led to the production of fertilisers and biogases that help generate higher revenues for farmers and productivity gains (Personal communication with Manuel Albaladejo, Head of UNIDO representative for Argentina, Chile, Uruguay and Paraguay, April 2021).

Another important question is that of the scope for state interventions in the process of climate-smart agriculture development. Valuable lessons can be drawn from the range of interventionist agricultural policies that were used in today's rich countries, both in terms of inputs policy (i.e. land policy, knowledge policy, credit policy, and physical inputs policy) and outputs policy (measures intended to increase farm income stability and the measures intended to improve agricultural marketing and processing) (Chang, 2009). The Brazilian experience in terms of climate smart agriculture also offers insightful lessons in terms of the role of policy instruments such as R&D policies and financial incentives. For instance, the Brazilian Agricultural Research Corporation (Embrapa) has been a critical public actor in the development of new crop varieties and farming techniques adapted to Brazil's diverse agro-ecological zones, which has helped improve productivity, reduce the environmental impact of agriculture, and increase resilience to climate change (Parente et al., 2021). Other flagship programmes include the Amazon Fund (launched in 2008) and Low-Carbon Agriculture Plan (launched in 2010), which included financial incentives for farmers to adopt practices such as integrated crop-livestock-forest systems, no-till farming, and the restoration of degraded pastures. Notwithstanding remaining challenges, Brazil's experience around climate-resilient agriculture bears high relevance that could form the basis of policy lessons for nations aiming to increase the resilience of their agriculture or diversify towards climate-resilient crops as part of a green economic transformation strategy.

Biodiverse Nations: Varieties of Nature-Based Services and Their Development Impact

For biodiverse nations, greening economic development faces an additional important consideration: the preservation and maintenance of local natural ecosystems. This issue is particularly relevant in Latin America, Central Africa, and Southeast Asia, which contain most of the planet's biodiversity hotspots. The interplay between a nation's biodiversity and economic activity has historically tipped in favour of resource extraction. Nevertheless, there are several ways in which the conservation of a country's biodiversity can support economic development, which explains the increasing attention devoted to bioeconomy strategies.[32] This section explores the extent to which different types of nature-based activities provide alternatives to deforestation and environmentally damaging extractive activities in regions seeking development while protecting their natural assets.

Market-Based Conservation Instruments and Their Limitations

Some nations are currently providing a range of ecosystem services (such as carbon storage, watershed protection, and conservation of fauna and flora) from which the whole world benefits and should compensate. In the past decades, several policy efforts were made to marketise and compensate for the protection of such valuable assets. For instance, Costa Rica's pioneering Payments for Environmental Services Program (PES) is a financial mechanism whereby landowners receive direct payments for the ecological services that their lands produce when they adopt environmentally friendly land uses and forest management techniques (Malavasi and Kellenberg, 2002). The advantage of those programmes is also that they enable to remunerate communities involved in conservation in remote areas and who have access to limited occupational choices. However, there have been criticisms on the degree of environmental additionally of PES and warnings regarding over-relying on them (Sierra and Russman, 2006; Muradian et al., 2013), Another concern is that PES mechanisms are often limited to national boundaries and local communities are not directly remunerated from the international community for this 'tradable' service. Linking this agenda with an international financing system is key to ensuring its long-term viability and environmental justice.

A similar logic applies to carbon markets: to be leveraged as a developmental strategy, carbon emissions trading systems need to cut across country boundaries to provide foreign exchange revenues to compensate for ecosystem services from international trade partners – rather than local actors exclusively. This agenda is of particular relevance for carbon-negative countries (namely Bhutan, Panama, and Suriname), where monetising ecosystem services represents a low-hanging fruit, as it requires relatively low financial investment while creating jobs and providing revenues in remote rural areas without compromising the national ecological agenda. However, considerable diplomatic policy efforts are required for the development of international carbon trading systems,

---

[32] The bioeconomy can be defined as 'the production, utilization and conservation of biological resources, including related knowledge, science, technology, and innovation, to provide information, products, processes and services in all economic sectors aiming toward a sustainable economy' (see International Advisory Council of the Global Bioeconomy Summit, 2018).

and to ensure that associated revenues provide opportunities for sustainable development rather than turning recipients into rentier states.

In that perspective, the REDD+ programme provides valuable lessons. Developed by Parties to the United Nations Framework Convention on Climate Change (UNFCCC), it aimed to provide finance for developing countries to contribute to climate change mitigation efforts in the forest sector. However, the programme has had mixed results and faced several criticisms (Massarella et al., 2018). One of the common issues relates to the size of the financial investments, which has been found to be below what is needed to disincentivise local communities from pursuing timber mining and other environmentally damaging activities (Overman et al., 2019). Other criticisms have been made both in terms of its environmental impact (especially in terms of carbon leakage) and its social impact (with issues of land grabbing by wealthy groups to reap REDD+ funding at the expense of indigenous communities), which has put into question the continuation of the programme and market-based conservation instruments more broadly (see Fletcher et al., 2016; Overman et al., 2019).

The Limits of Ecotourism as a Strategy for Conservation and Development

Ecotourism has also become increasingly popular across biodiverse nations as a way to promote environmentally friendly growth. It promotes responsible travel to natural areas while improving the well-being of local people. Ecotourism's appeal rests in its potential to provide local economic benefits while maintaining ecological resource integrity through low-impact, non-consumptive resource use (Stem et al., 2003). In many ways, nature-based tourism services can accelerate poverty alleviation, especially in remote areas where alternative sources of job creation are scarce while providing foreign exchange across several economic sectors, thereby supporting economic diversification (Hübler, 2019). For instance, in Latin America and the Caribbean, ecotourism generates around 3.5 million jobs, which is about 1.5 per cent of total employment (Saget et al., 2020).

Nevertheless, overreliance on ecotourism has also often posed important environmental and developmental risks. Ecotourism cannot be viewed as a benign, non-consumptive use of natural resources in biodiverse nations because scale influences tourism's negative impacts, and where ecotourism dominates local economies, towns may become economically vulnerable (Jacobson and Lopez, 1994). Besides offering limited prospects for quality job creation and economic upgrading (Lebdioui, 2022b), nature-based tourism activities are also likely to be most affected by climate change. For example, the 2017 hurricane season resulted in an estimated loss of more than 800,000 visitors to the Caribbean, which would have generated USD million for the region and supported about 11,000 jobs (Saget et al., 2020)

In Costa Rica and Ecuador, for instance, where ecotourism has gained prominence as a strategy to align both conservation and development, assessments of its impact have been mixed. On the one hand, some existing assessments reveal that the tourism industry tends to provide jobs with higher salaries, including for young people and women with children (Hunt et al., 2015). On the other hand, some negative impacts of the ecotourism industry including solid waste generation, air pollution, habitat destruction, sociocultural ills, as well as overdependence of fiscal revenues on external shocks affect ecotourism (Koens et al., 2009; Lebdioui, 2022b; Stem et al., 2003).

As a result, notwithstanding the benefits that ecotourism can provide on a limited scale, identifying alternative ways to capture the developmental value of biodiversity to complement – and at times supplement – ecotourism is critical in biodiverse nations aiming to promote conservation.

Biodiversity-Based Innovation Ecosystems: Overcoming the Northern Exploitation of Southern Biodiversity

Several economists have described the R&D process as one of information utilisation, application, and diffusion (e.g. Arrow, 1972) and dependent upon a stock of 'information' for its generation of useful innovations (Stoneman, 1983). Natural ecosystems also hold considerable value as a source of information that can feed into innovation processes (see Pearce and Pearce, 2001; Simpson et al., 1996; Swanson, 1996). As illustrated in Figure 11, there are two main ways in which the conservation of biodiversity holds value for innovation processes: as a provider of genetic material, through a process known as *bioprospecting*; as a source of inspiration for innovation, through a process known as *biomimicry*.

Northern-based industries heavily rely on southern-based biodiversity for R&D processes in various industries (Swanson, 1996). However, the informational value of biodiversity has often been extracted by foreign firms without recognition or compensation, which has given rise to an astonishing number of biopiracy cases in developing nations. Meanwhile, the biodiversity-based innovation sector has so far remained at an embryonic stage across biodiverse developing nations. There have been laudable efforts to leverage the innovation value of biodiversity, but those have mostly been limited to bioprospecting, which can be defined as a systematic and organised search for useful products derived from bioresources including plants, microorganisms, animals, and so on, which can be developed further for commercialisation and overall benefits of the society (Oyemitan, 2017). The most well-known initiative took place in the 1990s in

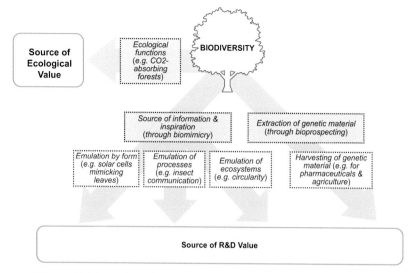

Figure 11 The value of biodiversity as an input into R&D processes
Source: Lebdioui (2022)

Costa Rica, with the creation of the National Biodiversity Institute (InBio), which worked under the premise that a country will be able to conserve a major portion of its wild biodiversity if this biodiversity generates enough intellectual and economic benefits to make up for its maintenance (Mateo et al., 2001). Nevertheless, serious doubts have been raised regarding the relative economic and developmental benefits of bioprospecting. This is well illustrated by some of the celebrated deals between InBio and foreign pharmaceutical companies, in which the royalties to be earned by Costa Rica should commercial drugs be developed are believed to be less than USD 1.1 million (Barrett and Lybbert, 2000). As a result, after three decades of activity, InBio ceased to operate due to the dried-up funding sources – 80 per cent of which came from the international community – and its inability to become financially sustainable.[33]

In contrast to using nature for extracting genetic material, biomimicry involves learning from and emulating biological forms, processes, and ecosystems tested by the environment and refined through evolution (Benyus, 1997). It marks a radical shift from the Industrial Revolution, which was 'an era based on what we can extract from nature' (Benyus, 1997), but it also helps overcome the scalability problem that often hinders nature-based solutions that require the availability of primary material extracted from nature (e.g. volcanic rocks for

---

[33] More recently, other initiatives to promote bio-innovation were launched in Costa Rica, such as the Biomaterials hub to promote R&D around biodiversity and sustainability.

carbon capture).[34] The field of biomimicry has been booming with a twelvefold increase in biomimicry patents and research grants over the past twenty years (see Fermanian Business & Economic Institute, 2020) and offers interesting prospects for leveraging local biodiversity as a factor endowment for innovation to 'leapfrog' towards high value-added sectors. However, very few public policies support its development in the developing world, which is paradoxical given that this is where most of the world's biodiversity is. As a result, the benefits of the biodiversity-based innovation sector (in terms of job gains and value creation) have mostly been captured by a handful of high-income indus-trialised economies in the Global North (Germany, South Korea, the United States, as well as France) where a range of publicly funded R&D programmes and grants have been implemented (see Lebdioui, 2022b).

Governments have a critical role to play in encouraging the transition towards knowledge-intensive biodiversity-based activities beyond mere rent maximisa-tion from resource exploitation, in line with the theoretical insights from the literature on national innovation ecosystems (Lee, 2013; Lundvall, 2016; Malerba, 2002; Nelson and Winter, 1982). Policy interventions in the biodiver-sity-based innovation sector are indeed justified given the existence of market imperfections and coordination failures (Lebdioui, 2022b). Those include finan-cing for physical, digital, and legal infrastructure to provide agents with more opportunities for both strategic and serendipitous nature-based innovation (i.e. through the creation of 'eco-labs' in biodiverse areas and digital repositories); streamlining of administrative processes for research permits to study biodiver-sity; and the promotion of integral and interdisciplinary education programmes in bio-innovation processes. Unlike many other 'traditional' sectors, biomim-icry heavily relies on a strategy mix of skills (such as biological knowledge but also chemistry, design, and engineering skills) to abstract biological strategies into applicable design to solve human challenges (Kennedy et al., 2015), and which the standard curriculums generally do not provide.

The Context of Fossil-Fuel Producers: Repurposing Capabilities for Green Diversification

Fossil-fuel producers are facing the headwinds of the global decarbonisation agenda, but this does not mean that they are condemned to be the losers of the global energy transition. To meet their dual energy transition and economic diversification needs, fossil-fuel-dependent economies may not necessarily

---

[34] Biomimicry can also support the broader conservation agenda if some conditions are met (for instance, biodiversity-based innovation practices need to be conducted in ways and on a scale that does not damage or disrupt fragile ecosystem (see Lebdioui, 2022b).

need to *ignore* their non-renewable resources as they can *leverage* them towards green economic transformation. This may sound counterintuitive, but fossil-fuel producers have acquired productive capabilities that can be repurposed in a wide range of green industrial sectors, especially with the help of the right policy tools. Here, I want to discuss three main stages (which we identify in Al Saffar and Lebdioui, forthcoming) that underpin developmental green economic diversification from the perspective of fossil-fuel-producing countries.

Stage 1: Energy Efficiency and Clean Energy Deployment as Fossil-Fuel Rent Maximisation Measures (Without Having to Extract More Fossil Fuels)

Many fossil-fuel-producing developing economies that have resisted the deployment of clean energies are consuming an increasingly large share of their fossil-fuel production, limiting their export capacity and associated rents. This is particularly relevant in the MENA region where oil and gas account for almost 95 per cent of electricity generation and where thermal plants consume more than one-third of gas production (Al Saffar and Wanner, 2022). Indonesia provides a cautionary tale: because of a surge in its domestic oil consumption, and though it is among the twenty-five largest oil producers worldwide, Indonesia became a net oil importer in 2004, which prompted its exit from the Organization of the Petroleum Exporting Countries .

In such contexts, deploying clean energies and improving energy efficiency (through the use of more efficient gas turbines, or by reducing gas flaring, for instance) can help reduce domestic oil and gas consumption, and therefore free up more fossil-fuel resources for exports (without the additional risk of stranded assets associated with upstream investment). This strategy represents a low-hanging fruit to generate more capital that can be invested for diversification in fossil-fuel-dependent economies, without even requiring an increase in fossil-fuel production.

Stage 2: Reinvesting Rents Towards New Productive Capabilities to Break the Rentier Model

Fossil-fuel producers, particularly those with high fossil-fuel rents per capita, generally have access to greater financial resources compared to resource-poor countries, which could, in theory, help them finance productive investments for climate-resilient economic diversification and overcome hurdles such as the high cost of capital for clean energy investment. However, the decision to invest in green industrialisation is influenced by a combination of factors that go beyond fiscal capacity alone, and include political will, strategic foresight, external pressures, as well as institutional capabilities for domestic investments.

In that sense, the standard policy advice of resource wealth management, which has been dominated by a short-term fiscal stabilisation agenda, will not suffice in the face of the pressing need for economic diversification (Chang and Lebdioui, 2020). To stimulate a long-term, climate-resilient structural transformation that also reduces exposure to transition risks, resource revenue management strategies need to tackle the root causes of fossil-fuel dependence (insufficiently diversified productive structures) rather than solely addressing its symptoms (e.g. vulnerability to commodity price volatility). Therefore, rather than solely sticking to investing fossil-fuel rents in a fiscal stabilisation fund, policymakers may find it more effective to capitalise sovereign development funds or a national development bank, provided they have clear mandates, strong governance, legislative oversight, and – not least – proper investment analysis, monitoring, and evaluation (Addison and Lebdioui, 2022).

Though economically sensible, the idea of reinvesting fossil-fuel rents for green economic transformation is paved with several political challenges, including resistance from powerful elites that have a vested interest in maintaining the status quo, and institutional inertia, which explains why countries might not have managed to diversify in the first place. A productive management of resource rent can be quite politically challenging as it disrupts the traditional dynamics of the rentier state model. For instance, in most of the MENA region, the political economy of oil rents has been characterised by weak productive constituencies and institutional arrangements entirely predicated on the uninterrupted flow of oil rents rather than resilient governance mechanisms (Malik, 2019). Reinvesting fossil-fuel rents therefore requires new elite bargains and carefully crafted incentives for fossil-fuel actors by making alternatives more viable and competitive, as well as an acute understanding of the role that they can play in the transition, which relates to the stage 3 strategy.

Stage 3: Repurposing Transversal Capabilities in Oil and Gas Extraction Towards Clean Energy Supply Chain Integration

Throughout history, nations and firms have kept up with technological disruptions by repurposing their capabilities transversally, from Nokia repurposing its logging industry expertise towards telecommunications; Slack Technologies leveraging the internal communication platform they developed while in the gaming industry to enter the business communication industry; or 3 M evolving from a small-scale mining venture to a highly diversified conglomerate with innovative products such as Post-it Notes and Scotch tape. The technological linkages between different products might not always be obvious. For instance, producing rifles creates a capacity for producing other things such as sewing machines, bicycles, and automobiles (Rosenberg, 1976).

In the fossil-fuel sector, the ability to leverage transversal capabilities bears considerable implications for economic diversification and macroeconomic resilience. For instance, in Malaysia, several suppliers in the oil and gas sector have managed to acquire transversal skills that contributed to sectors beyond the petroleum industry.[35] Such transversal skills have proven particularly useful after the collapse in oil prices in 2014, which incentivised Malaysian suppliers to mitigate their reliance on the broader fossil-fuel sector (Lebdioui, 2019). In the context of the dual challenge of diversification and energy transition, a repurposing agenda entails the exploitation of existing knowledge, infrastructure, and technologies involved in fossil-fuel production towards integrating value chains that are central to the green economy. At the corporate level, many oil and gas companies have already started to reposition themselves to take advantage of new opportunities arising out of the low-carbon economy, both to improve their financial resilience and corporate image.

Analysing how those businesses have started to repurpose some of their in-house capabilities towards clean energy operations, it is possible to identify a range of technological, organisational and infrastructure linkages between petroleum extraction and clean energy production (see Lebdioui and Bilek, forthcoming). To name a few examples, activities such as chemical and temperature engineering services can be easily repurposed towards green hydrogen production, oil and gas reservoirs can be reconverted for carbon storage, and the construction and maintenance of offshore oil platforms involve a range of technological capabilities that can serve the construction of offshore wind platforms, while petroleum refineries can be repurposed as biofuel refineries (Lebdioui and Bilek, forthcoming).

However, not all activities have the same scope for repurposing. For instance, capabilities such as drilling expertise and equipment do not offer great degrees of linkages with clean energy production, implying that workers with those skills will require considerable retraining as part of a low-carbon energy future, making the role of reskilling and labour market policy interventions particularly important. Promoting a socially inclusive repurposing of capabilities from fossil fuels to hydrogen supply chains development requires a multi-dimensional and proactive policy approach, along with careful coordination of energy policy, fiscal policy, industrial policy, skills development policy, as well as labour market policy. Policymakers may find it useful to create a national agency with a skills repurposing mission and retraining capacity to help acquire the skills and know-how required for local integration in different green industries, and the creation of a national readiness framework in the context of the energy transition.

---

[35] Firms initially providing oil fluids engineering and drilling waste management services have also managed to develop globally competitive railway and nuclear centrifuge engineering capabilities.

Though they refer to very distinct processes and policy strategies, the three stages are mutually reinforcing. However, the combination, sequencing, and scale at which those pathways can be pursued differs from country to country depending on the local context.

Size and Neighbourhood Matters: Economies of Scale, Market Piggybacking, and Supply Chain Regionalisation

Not all countries can achieve green industrialisation through demand-led growth. To date, some of the most successful adopters of green industrial opportunities have been extremely large economies (in terms of domestic market size), such as China, the USA, Brazil, the EU, and India. In smaller economies where the domestic market demand is often not large enough to reach economies of scale, green economic transformation requires access to another country's larger market demand, but also multilateral coordination towards regional developmentalism.

The idea of 'piggy-backing' on a larger and/or more economically prosperous neighbouring country's demand as an industrial development strategy is not new: Vietnam, Poland, and Mexico have provided useful cases over the past few decades.[36] It is also in that perspective that Mexico stands to benefit from the recent low-carbon technology market push in the United States. The IRA, which took effect in 2022, provides generous tax credits for electric vehicles sold in the United States and mandates that a certain percentage of the battery components be assembled or manufactured in North America (or countries with whom the USA has a free trade agreement). Such policies have already led to new investments in Mexico, whose ability to benefit from the IRA is not only a function of geographic proximity but also the market access allowed by the United States-Mexico-Canada Agreement, the presence of low-wage skilled labour as well as domestic capabilities to attract investments in low-carbon technology supply chains (especially in the automotive sector). The ability to tap into another country's market is indeed conditioned by several factors (including signed trade agreements, domestic capabilities, geographic proximity, and transportation costs). But in the long term, a country's success in seizing opportunities stemming from another country's market demand also hinges on the use of industrial policies to improve supply-side industrial capabilities, such as the development of a skilled local workforce capable of engaging in high-value-added industries to move beyond the mere assembly and processing activities, and implementing improvements in

---

[36] For instance, Vietnam's proximity to China has allowed it to tap into the Chinese supply chain and cater to its immense market demand, especially as labour costs in China have risen.

logistics and infrastructure (both digital and physical) that are essential to attracting investments in high value-added industries.

However, this strategy is not without its risks. Heavy dependence on a single market can expose a country to economic vulnerabilities if there's a downturn or radical policy change in the larger country. Diplomatic tensions can also affect the ability of a country to rely on another country's demand as an engine of growth. Market diversification and strategic planning are essential to mitigate these risks. It is also crucial to ensure that this strategy aligns with the long-term domestic developmental goals, rather than locking countries in unsustainable development routes (e.g. water-intensive industrial or agricultural production in areas at high risk of water stress to cater to external demand, such as avocado production in Chile or green hydrogen production in North Africa). Furthermore, not all nations have access to large neighbouring markets to bolster their green economic transformation (for instance, most Central and Latin American nations do not benefit from the same conditions as Mexico in terms of privileged and low-cost access to the vast U.S. market). Recent evidence reveals that, except in Mexico, limited nearshoring to the region has taken place so far (Pietrobelli and Seri, 2023). Countries surrounded by smaller economies therefore face a collective demand-side challenge. In regions like Africa, the Caribbean, and Central and South America, where individual markets may be limited (except for Brazil), relying on external demand might not always be viable as a development strategy, and regional integration is critical to ensure the coordination and perennity of demand-side policies.[37]

That said, regional integration is not an easy task (see Heine, 2012; Ocampo, 2006). Political and ideological differences, external influences, and gaps in physical infrastructure connectivity, as well as disparities in economic development levels among neighbouring countries, can generate resistance to regional integration. Latin America is a case in point, where the numerous efforts to promote regional integration have mostly failed in previous decades (Merke et al., 2021). Despite these challenges, many regions around the world have successfully pursued various levels of integration (such as the EU, Association of Southeast Asian Nations (ASEAN), and the African Union, among others), which can serve as the basis for useful lessons. One of those is that regional integration is not just about trade but about increased social and economic development (Stiglitz, 2016). For instance, an important step towards regional integration in Africa has been taken with the signing of the African Continental Free Trade Area (AfCFTA) in March 2018, but in

---

[37] See discussion on what subregional trade agreements have meant for regional integration Latin America in Salazar-Xirinachs (2002).

many ways, the challenge of regionalising supply chains and increased demand-side coordination remains.

To understand the full scope of regional cooperation in the context of green economic transformation, it is useful to go beyond the linear approach to regional integration as developed by Viner (1950), which consists of a trade liberalisation approach to integration whereby countries first adopt free trade areas, then customs unions, and then common markets. In contrast to the linear approach, several scholars have put forward the notion of 'developmental regional integration' (or at least different variations of the concept, see Adejumobi and Kreiter, 2020; Davies, 1996; Ismail, 2018; UNCTAD, 2013). This approach to regional integration emphasises macro- and micro-coordination in a multi-sectoral programme embracing production, infrastructure, and trade, notably to build regional value chains that can foster industrial transformation, especially for small economies (Davies, 1996; Ismail, 2018). Adopting a 'developmental regionalist' approach in the African context, Ismail (2022) outlines how the AfCFTA can be implemented in a manner that supports the transformative industrialisation of Africa and facilitates a 'climate-resilient developmental regionalism'.

Building on the idea of 'climate-resilient developmental regionalism', we can put forward different mechanisms that help coordinate demand-side and supply-side policies at the regional level. Besides the mere existence of regional free trade agreements, 'climate-resilient developmental regionalism' can take the form of regional strategies for specific low-carbon industries to help align demand-side policies to create larger and more stable regional market demand. On the supply-side, developmental regional integration mechanisms span a wide spectrum: from knowledge-sharing on critical material supplies and region-wide certification for low-carbon products to pooling limited R&D resources for joint innovation to shared challenges (such as high-altitude mining in the Andean region or developing solar plant equipment that is resilient to the Sahara's extreme temperatures).

It is also worth highlighting that, besides building a larger common market, the potential of regional integration is more than the sum of its parts. This is why 'green' regional developmentalism is also based on the idea that neighbouring countries leverage their complementary assets (whether it is critical mineral abundance, manufacturing capacity, renewable energy potential, as well as proximity to important trade routes) to develop an efficient regional industrial ecosystem around climate-related technologies.

In practice, achieving green regional developmentalism remains paved with challenges, especially in terms of financing and political alignment (and particularly so in Africa and Latin America), but surmounting such challenges is necessary, given the significant development opportunities and challenges that arise in the twenty-first century for some of the world's regions.

6 Kicking Away the 'Green' Ladder: Green Protectionism, Broken Pledges, and Double Trade Standards

> The present approach towards the poor is very much tilted in favour of palliative economics [...] alleviating the symptoms of poverty, rather than attacking its real causes. This creates a system of 'welfare colonialism' increasing the dependence of poor countries, thereby hindering, rather than promoting, long-term structural change.
>
> — Erik Reinert

The Rise of Green Protectionism in Industrialised Nations

Climate change knows no borders. A few countries are disproportionately responsible for causing it by appropriating more than their fair share of the atmospheric commons, while those that suffer the worst consequences tend to be developing nations that contributed the least to climate change (Hickel, 2020). However, as explained in Section 3, instead of honouring their climate responsibilities, the world's major economies' response to climate change has mostly consisted in providing a competitive advantage to domestic firms to capture the industrial benefits that arise from decarbonisation. The green resurgence of industrial policy, even in the United States, is motivated by the recognition that the low-carbon transition offers significant green windows of opportunity that must be seized by moving early (Lema et al., 2020), but also by geostrategic interests to reduce China's low-carbon technology dominance (White House, 2023).

The US is not alone in promoting green protectionism. In 2023, the EU also implemented its CBAM, which initially applies to imports of certain goods (such as cement, iron, and steel, aluminium, fertilisers, electricity, and hydrogen). While it has been framed as a climate action, concerns have arisen that it is a de-facto import constraint, which can be interpreted as violating several provisions under the General Agreement on Tariffs and Trade (GATT). Regardless of its legality, the EU's CBAM is a source of concern for developing countries as it could impose costs on their exporters, including in Africa, where it could cause a GDP loss of $31 billion (Aggad and Luke, 2023; Usman et al., 2021).

The main defence in terms of the development impact of green industrial policy tools used in the global north has consisted in the idea that those interventions will reduce the cost of low-carbon technologies, making low-carbon transitions more attractive in poor countries. There is validity in this argument, but the policy strategies currently undertaken by the world's major economies (whether it is the United States, the EU, or China) mostly constrain the role of developing regions as sources of raw materials to fuel the low-carbon technological revolution, thereby reproducing the trade dependencies that have undermined global development in the past century (see Radley for an analysis in the case of the Congo).

Some parallels can therefore be drawn between the emergence of green industrial policy and the past, and it comes to the international division of labour and the international political economy of catching-up. Reviving some of the ideas of the nineteenth century German economist Friederich List, Ha-Joon Chang (2002) argued that rich nations have a tendency to 'kick away the ladder' by which they climb up, in order to deprive others of the means of climbing up after them. This seems to remain true in the context of green economic development models. While green protectionism might seem like a reasonable response to safeguard domestic industries in their low-carbon transition, the way 'green' industrial policies have been enacted by the world's major economies fails to address the fundamental challenge of a just transition. Through their green protectionism, rich nations are effectively breaking the central promise of the UN sustainable development goals of leaving no one behind.[38] This begs the questions: is green industrial policy inevitably protectionist and discriminatory? How to balance the regained popularity of industrial policy as an opportunity for global development while avoiding the pitfalls of green protectionism from the Global North? Is green industrial policy fairer when it focuses on the creation of markets (see Mazzucato, 2015, 2016; Perez, 2016) rather than import constraint measures? The rest of this section looks at the ways the tensions between the green industrial policy and international trade rules, the uneven financing landscape for green economic transformation, before exploring some ways forward.

Double Standards of the International Trade System and the WTO's Contested Relevance

Developing countries need adequate policy space to pursue industrial policies to accelerate their green economic transformation and ensure the sustainability of their development. But to what extent is the pursuit of green industrial policy possible within the current rules of the world trade system? Already in 2014, Mark Wu and James Salzman had anticipated the next generation of trade and environmental conflicts as a result of the emergence of green industrial policy (Wu and Salzman, 2014). The attempt by some countries to pursue green industrial policies has at times violated World Trade Organization (WTO)

---

[38] Ghosh et al. (2023) even argues that the insufficient actions from rich countries are leading to a new form of climate imperialism.

rules and international trade agreements, especially around tariffs, local content requirements, and intellectual property rights. This was the case for India in 2013, when the United States government (ironically using the same policy tools today) filed a complaint regarding the domestic content requirements under the Jawaharlal Nehru National Solar Mission for solar cells and solar modules (WTO, 2018). Governments, in responding to negative rulings, either find legal work-around solutions (especially those with more technical resources to navigate or bend trade rules) or sever only the quasi-protectionist elements of their green industrial policies (while trying to keep the environmental benefits in place in most cases) (Wu and Salzman, 2014). Furthermore, the policy space for trade-related environmental measures is safeguarded under GATT Article XX(b) where 'WTO members may adopt policy measures that are inconsistent with GATT disciplines, but necessary to protect human, animal or plant life or health or relating to the conservation of exhaustible natural resources'.[39]

However, in practice, the use of this article is far from straightforward and has rarely been effective due to a two-step evaluation weighing the legitimacy of the environmental policy challenged against its potential negative impact on trade and the extent to which it constitutes a discriminatory or disguised restriction on international trade (Wu and Salzman, 2013). When measures overtly favoured domestic products over imports, WTO panels and the Appellate Body (which has ceased to function since 2019 after the appointment of its new members was blocked by the United States) have generally declined to uphold the defendants' invocation of the so-called environmental and other public interest exceptions (Tucker and Meyer, 2022).

However, some governments have been resourceful at circumventing trade rules, especially by disguising their industrial policies under the umbrella of climate action. The EU is a case in point, revealing the extent to which protectionist motives can trump ecological goals in trade negotiations. Seeking to promote its biofuel production by preventing the imports of lower-cost biodiesel from Southeast Asia and South America, the EU has implemented duties on biodiesel imports that were later deemed illegal by the WTO (Tucker and Meyer, 2022:125). The EU subsequently resorted to using environmental regulations arguing that palm oil-based biofuel did not comply with its renewable energy targets, prompting disputes from Indonesia and Malaysia on the grounds that the EU's palm oil restrictions are discriminatory). However, at the same time, the EU has often also restricted the imports of goods

---

[39] See General Agreement on Tariffs and Trade art. XX, Oct. 30, 1947, 61 Stat. A-11, 55 U.N.T. S.194 (hereinafter GATT).

that could enable it to meet its climate targets. A famous sticking point in the negotiations on the Environmental Goods Agreement (a multilateral effort within the WTO to liberalise tariffs on environmental goods) was the case of bicycles. While the Chinese government argued that a bicycle constitutes an environmental good because it is an emissions-free form of transportation, the EU negotiators were reluctant to liberalise tariffs on bicycles for fear that a large influx of foreign-produced lower-cost bicycles would damage EU bicycle producers (Benson, 2023). The Environmental Goods Agreement negotiations have broken down as a result. More recently, concerns have been raised regarding the legality of the EU's CBAM, which several developing nations are planning to challenge at the WTO.

If powerful nations can bend – or deliberately not comply with – trade rules, the purpose of the WTO in the age of ecological crises must be questioned. In many ways, the rise of green industrial policies and green protectionism complicates the balance between trade liberalisation and environmental protection agendas. There are reasons to believe that the recent adoption of explicitly protectionist policies in the United States (such as the IRA and the CHIPS Act) may make global trade rules obsolete, leaving some policy space to late industrialisers. As rich nations often manage to bend trade rules to their advantage, it also provides precedents for developing countries to pursue the same strategies. The future relevance of the WTO may depend on its ability to adapt to – and address – this challenge. At the same time, notwithstanding the restrictions that the WTO places, they also leave governments some degree of flexibility to adopt some green industrial policies, with various exceptions and special treatments. In contrast, regional, multilateral, and bilateral agreements are typically even more restrictive on industrial policy space than WTO rules.

Of particular concern is the Investor-State Dispute Settlement (ISDS) scheme, which is included in many trade and investment agreements and represents a major obstacle to green economic transformation as it enables transnational corporations to use legal action against governments in courts outside of the national legal system over the implementation of sustainability measures that threaten their profits. Fossil-fuel companies are therefore taking advantage of the ISDS scheme to sue over fossil-fuel phase-out plans and have sued governments across the world for £18 billion as climate policies threaten their profits (Global Justice Now, 2021). The ISDS scheme is particularly threatening to the implementation of sustainability measures and broader green economic policy in developing countries (Tienhaara, 2018), where foreign polluting industries have been relocated and have much fewer resources to fight legal battles outside of their jurisdictions. Countries such as South Africa, India, New Zealand, Bolivia, Tanzania, Canada, and the US have all taken steps towards getting rid of ISDS (Limb, 2022). But more efforts are needed in that direction to put an end to the use of ISDS in contexts in which it jeopardises the global fight against climate change and the achievement of sustainability goals more broadly.

Bridging the Financing Gap to Support Green Economic Transformation: How Credible are Rich Nations?

Green economic transformation and industrial policy require a mobilisation of resources, especially in least income countries that face higher infrastructure gaps, external borrowing costs, and stricter financial constraints to spend on productivity-enhancing assets. In theory, climate financing can help bridge this gap. However, despite the rhetoric used by world leaders summit after summit, the climate financing landscape is appalling and exacerbates the impact of green trade protectionism. Rich nations have even broken their promise (made at the 2009 UN climate summit in Copenhagen) to channel a total of USD 100 billion a year to poor nations by 2020 to help them adapt to climate change and mitigate further rises in temperature. The United States provided less than a fifth of what they should have paid ($7.6 billion out of $40 billion), while Australia, Canada, and the UK also fell far short of what they should have contributed (Timperley, 2021). This was not even a hard target to reach: $100 billion represents a fraction of what governments spent to bail out banks in the aftermath of the 2008–2009 financial crisis.[40] To further put things into perspective, while failing to fulfil its $40 billion climate financing pledge, the United States government spent a staggering $1.5 trillion to manufacture the rarely used F-35 Fighter jet, one of the most expensive weapons systems in history. Meanwhile, the EU has allocated over 1 trillion euros in sustainable investments over a decade, but the amount of climate funds from the European Commission and the European Investment Bank (EIB; the EU's lending arm) to developing countries has not increased from an average of around 5.7 billion euros ($6.7 billion) since 2018 (Usman et al., 2021).

Beyond the missed targets in terms of climate financing, attention must also be drawn to *the type* of climate finance provision to date. Rather than supporting green economic transformation, most climate financing has consisted of non-concessional loans over grant financing and focused on funding climate mitigation initiatives over climate adaptation and resilience (Colenbrander et al., 2022; Usman et al., 2021). Considering their economic needs and different

---

[40] The UK government alone provided £123.93 billion to support banks (with the total amount pledged exceeding £1 trillion), while the US federal government used around $245 billion in taxpayer money to bail out banks (The Guardian, 2011; US Department of the Treasury, 2016).

responsibilities in the context of the climate crisis, developing countries need a lot more financing not merely to import low-carbon technologies but to support local climate-resilient economic transformations.

Reclaiming Policy Space for Green Economic Transformation

Several initiatives have emerged in recent years to redraw the global finance and trade landscape in a way that brings equity to the climate and development agenda. The one that has received the most attention to date is the *Bridgetown Initiative*, put forward by the Prime Minister of Barbados, Mia Mottley, which proposes the rechannelling of unused International Monetary Fund (IMF) special drawing rights to developing countries; adding climate resilience debt clauses in new loans by the IFIs; and providing $100 billion in foreign exchange guarantees to help reduce currency risks and, by extension, the cost of capital for renewable energy projects in developing countries.

Notwithstanding the major improvements of the global financial system that the Bridgetown Initiative entails, the agenda of promoting productive resilience to climate and transition risks also requires revisiting trade rules that are restricting the use of green industrial policies in developing nations and consolidating the technological dependence of the global south to the global north. Rather than seeing global decarbonisation as an economic race, rich industrialised nations must recognise the value of inclusive green industrial policies in developing nations and actively support their efforts. Rather than relying on punitive measures, Ismail (2022) suggests that developed economies such as the EU and the United States that are considering applying CBAMs against imports from developing countries should rather support a positive trade agenda to encourage and assist developing countries to implement their mitigation commitments and adaptation development strategies. An alternative could also be for the EU and the US to share some of the income earned through applying this levy with the countries negatively affected by it and do so in a way that supports the latter's climate resilience.

This support can take various forms, such as technical and financial assistance for green productive capabilities accumulation and resilience (in other words, climate financing beyond palliative solutions and climate mitigation); further commitment for low-carbon technology transfer (which is at the core of the UNFCCC), notably by increasing support to institutions such as the Global Environment Facility, which, since its inception in 1991, has been financing the transfer of climate change-related and other environmentally sound technologies to developing countries.[41] International agreements should also further

---

[41] Technology transfer can be referred as 'a broad set of processes covering the flows of know-how, experience and equipment for mitigating and adapting to climate change amongst different

encourage cooperation with – and accountability from – the private sector to support low-carbon technology transfer and innovation cooperation in developing countries.

To expand their shrinking policy space for greening their productive structures, developing countries could also benefit from ending the use of the ISDS system against environmental regulations (which 400 civil society organisations are already calling for, Limb, 2022). Furthermore, to ensure that the development agenda of developing countries is not overburdened with a cost of carbon that exceeds their climate responsibilities, we must move towards a fair differentiation of carbon prices so that rich nations pay much more per CO_2 emitted than developing countries. Differentiated prices of carbon must not be solely based on purchasing power parity (as suggested in Lenain, 2023) but also reflect different climate responsibilities based on a country's historic contribution to GHG emissions. To further support the notion of the principle of common but differentiated responsibilities, the WTO could also use the example of the Doha Ministerial Declaration on the Trade-Related Aspects of Intellectual Property Rights (TRIPS) Agreement and Public Health to also expand TRIPS flexibilities for developing countries to climate-related goods (Ismail, 2022).

Those measures should not be considered a handout to developing nations. If we are to successfully fight against climate change, developing countries (which represent 99 per cent of projected global population growth but have much lower responsibility to mitigate climate change) will also need serious incentives to embark on more ecologically sustainable pathways. However, as is the case with climate and green industrial policy (which spans across various issues such as trade, climate, energy, and finance), institutional gridlocks arise where there are no effective means for coordinating all the bodies that can contribute to dealing with interconnected issues (Hale et al., 2013).Therefore, to move the needle and push for reforms in global trade and environmental rules that typically favour developed nations, developing nations and their international partners will need to build strong coalitions and engage in strategic collective actions in various fronts and forums, such as the WTO, and the Conference of the Parties, and International Finance Institutions.

Furthermore, in the era of a bipolar world, opportunities exist to leverage heightened geopolitical competition between the United States and China. As both superpowers seek to increase their spheres of influence, developing countries can strategically position themselves to leverage this rivalry to their

stakeholders such as governments, private sector entities, financial institutions, non-governmental organizations and research/education institutions' (IPCC, 2000).

advantage, especially in terms of low-carbon technology transfer. In Malay folklore, this is what is often referred to as the mouse-deer strategy, and it has defined ASEAN diplomacy in recent decades.[42] While China has already embarked on a global infrastructure development strategy through its Belt and Road Initiative with projects in Africa, Asia, and Latin America, there is scope for opening avenues for low-carbon technology transfer and cooperation for low-carbon technological innovation, adaptation, and diffusion, especially in light of China's technological dominance in this area (see Section 3). Meanwhile, the United States, in its efforts to counterbalance China's influence and catch up in low-carbon technology sectors, might be persuaded to offer more favourable terms for technology transfers, productive investments, and capacity-building programmes in developing countries. The recent U.S.-DRC-Zambia memorandum of understanding is a case in point as it demonstrates how the United States aims to counter China and bolster its clean energy supply chains by deepening ties with African nations (Soulé, 2023).

In sum, the road to socially inclusive and developmental global decarbonisation is paved with obstacles and cannot be achieved without expanding policy space for green economic transformation in developing nations. Important conversations on how to reform the global financial architecture to foster climate solidarity and resilience have begun, but progress has been slow. Furthermore, this agenda cannot happen without a parallel major rethinking of the global trade rules. And for the multilateral system to provide the coordination needed for shared prosperity and to fight climate change, we need better collective action and honest conversations about green industrial policy and green protectionism.

7 Conclusion and Reflections on the Future Relevance of Development Economics

> Each generation must, out of relative obscurity, discover its mission, fulfill it, or betray it.
>
> — Frantz Fanon

This Element aims to show the extent to which the conditions for economic development have been reframed in the context of a century that is marked by ecological challenges. The carbon-intensive economic models pursued in the past by now-rich countries are not likely to pay off, but policymakers will remain tempted to follow the well-trodden path of such models in the absence of

---

[42] As brought to my attention by Tan Sri Azman Mokhtar, the mouse deer – known as Kancil in Malay – occupies an important place as a trickster in Malay folklore and is used as an example of how a small animal can intelligently gain the necessary benefits from larger ones.

innovative and bold policy ideas to sustain livelihoods in an ecologically responsible way. Reimagining development is no easy thing, but the process of economic development has always been a dynamic one. Far from a logic of permanence, and similarly to how species evolve in nature, societies have throughout history adapted and reinvented their pathways to prosperity in response to various challenges, and the current environmental crisis is no exception. This process might be difficult to conceive for many, which is why policymaking requires a dose of creativity (or what Hirschman called the 'hiding hand') to overcome the many challenges – both known and unknown – that persist in achieving the vision of a sustainable future. By using their creative resources, countries can also trailblaze new green economic transformation paths that align with their unique circumstances and strengths.

Contrary to the perception that greening the economic structure is solely a rich country's mission, this Element also aims to show that adapting to avoid perishing also concerns poor nations. Governments, especially those in rich nations, are increasingly conscious of the economic opportunities stemming from the sustainability agenda and are increasingly adopting green industrial policies and protectionist policies in low-carbon industries. A major concern that arises is ensuring that global decarbonisation supports – rather than operates at the expense of – global development. To date, the ridiculously low resources devoted to climate financing and the high costs of capital for renewable energy projects in developing countries hinder the ability of policymakers to develop corridors of green industrialisation in developing economies (Lopes, 2022). If we are serious about our commitment to uplift people, communities, and nations out of the poverty trap, a major rethinking of climate financing and global trade rules is needed to level the playing field for green industrialisation opportunities.

While we should stress the inadequacy of climate financing, it must be emphasised that there is still some room left to disrupt the status quo through domestic measures to promote green economic transformation. In that perspective, the main messages of this Element are that green industrial policies can help countries develop productive capabilities for new structural transformation, but the suitability of different types of industrial policies is highly context-specific and conditioned by institutional constraints, existing state–business relations, and the stability of political systems. Furthermore, there are various possible pathways to green economic transformation. While drawing lessons from international experiences can be helpful, countries need to acknowledge and embrace their distinctive starting points and needs in their search for more resilient economic development models. For instance, while several nations are competing in low-carbon manufacturing, biodiverse regions may find it more appealing to focus on fostering nature-based innovation systems rather than unsustainably pursuing deforestation to make room for wind turbine factories.

The findings of this Element bear considerable policy implications. The process of green economic transformation is far too important and far too urgent to be left to markets alone. Governments will need to play a key role in implementing public policies that go beyond simply fixing market failure and instead shape the productive accumulation of capabilities to promote new activities that offer the best prospect of ensuring climate-resilient livelihoods. The role of industrial policy is of paramount importance in that regard but needs to be integrated within a wider joined-up policy approach to avoid policy inconsistencies. In many countries that do not have the large market size that China, Brazil, the EU, or the USA have, there is a limit to what government can achieve through industrial policy without regional cooperation.

The new environmental and economic realities also influence the pertinent research questions that development economists should be addressing to ensure their discipline is focused on present and future challenges. While we have seen improvements to rectify errors of *omission* in recent years, notably in terms of integrating environmental costs into economic calculations (e.g. the Stern review and the Dasgupta Review), our attention has been less focused on errors of *commission*. Firstly, the prevailing metrics of progress (such as GDP) still fail to account for present and future vulnerability to climate and transition risks. Even governments that are vocal about environmental crises face intense pressure from their constituents and international lenders to deliver GDP growth every year, regardless of the direction of such growth. Secondly, adapting economics to our climatic realities requires rethinking traditional development models by granting more value to *purpose* in economics research. Economics as a discipline may inevitably fail the world on climate and development if the brightest minds are only incentivised to answer questions that have a quantifiable and methodologically complex (and often obvious) answers rather than the difficult (and even existential) questions that may not allow for an answer that contains a precise number. Third, to improve our understanding of green structural transformation, future research needs to address some important blind spots, including:

(1) *The distributional effects of green industrial policy, globally and domestically.* This Element has focused on how decarbonisation stands to increase economic disparities between nations. But the industrial policy agenda, without proper safeguards, can also increase economic disparities within countries. This Element has focused on how decarbonisation stands to

increase economic disparities between nations, but the industrial policy agenda, without proper safeguards, can also increase inequality within countries, with some inevitable losers.

(2) *The role of civil society in green industrial policymaking*, not only to provide a watchdog mechanism to balance conflicting interests and benefit-sharing but also to ensure continuity and adjustments in democratic systems of governments where political leaders do not stay in power very long. Understanding the role of different actors in influencing the time horizon of the formulation of industrial policies can improve the balance between quick wins and long-term change.

(3) *The role of industrial policy for 'dematerialisation' and the reduction of waste.* While most of the attention is devoted to industrial policy in the context of low-carbon industries, another major environmental challenge remains under-studied: material contamination, which threatens our environment but also human livelihoods. Reducing humanity's material pollution indeed requires designing and manufacturing products to last longer, which stands in stark contrast with the logic of planned obsolescence. However, the literature on the economics of product durability remains surprisingly scant.

The path to greening economic development is paved with hurdles and complexities that demand an unparalleled level of political dedication at local, national, and global levels. But it is by achieving this level of commitment that we can really begin to pave the way for a new era of prosperity for both current and future generations. In the face of such critical urgency, economists and policymakers alike will have to adapt to this vital concern for sustainability and recognise its effects on dynamics of structural transformation. The message is unequivocal: we must either adapt to these evolving realities (and embrace the opportunities they present) or face the consequences of inaction.

References

Acemoglu, D., Aghion, P., Bursztyn, L., & Hemous, D. (2012). The environment and directed technical change. *American Economic Review, 102*(1), 131–166.

Addison, T. (2018). Climate change and the extractives sector. In T. Addison, & A. Roe, eds., *Extractive Industries: The Management of Resources as a Driver of Sustainable Development.* Oxford: Oxford University Press, p. 768.

Addison, T., & Lebdioui, A. (2022). *Public Savings in Africa: Do Sovereign Wealth Funds Serve Development?* United Nations University, World Institute for Development Economics Research.

Adejumobi, S., & Kreiter, Z. (2020). The theory and discourse of developmental regionalism. In S/ Adejumobi & C. Obi, eds., *Developmental Regionalism and EconomicTransformation in Southern Africa* (1st ed.). New York: Routledge. https://doi.org/10.4324/9781351053570.

Aggad, F., & Luke, D. (2023). *Implications for African Countries of a Carbon Border Adjustment Mechanism in the EU.* LSE and African Climate Foundation.

Aghion, P., Hepburn, C., Teytelboym, A., & Zenghelis, D. (2019). Path dependence, innovation and the economics of climate change. In R. Fouquet, ed., *Handbook on Green Growth.* Cheltenham: Edward Elgar Publishing. pp. 67–83.

Aiginger, K. (2015). Industrial policy for a sustainable growth path. In D. Bailey, K. Cowling, & P. Tomlinson, eds., *New Perspectives on Industrial Policy for a Modern Britain.* Oxford: Oxford University Press, pp. 365–394.

Al Jazeera. (2021). 'Chile's desert dumping ground for fast fashion leftovers'. 8 November, www.aljazeera.com/gallery/2021/11/8/chiles-desert-dumping-ground-for-fast-fashion-leftovers.

Al Saffar, A., & Wanner, B. (2022). How producers in the Middle East and North Africa can free up more natural gas for exports. *IEA Commentary.* 25 May, www.iea.org/commentaries/how-producers-in-the-middle-east-and-north-africa-can-free-up-more-natural-gas-for-exports.

Albaladejo, M. (2020). *Industrialization in Latin America: Exile and Return.* Vienna: UNIDO.

Altenburg, T., & Rodrik, D. (2017). Green industrial policy: Accelerating structural change towards wealthy green economies. *Green Industrial Policy.*

Ameli, N., Dessens, O., Winning, M., et al. (2021). Higher cost of finance exacerbates a climate investment trap in developing economies. *Nature Communications, 12*(1), 4046.

Amsden, A. H. (1989). *Asia's Next Giant: South Korea and Late Industrialization.* New York: Oxford University Press.

Anadon, L. D., Chan, G., Harley, A. G., et al. (2016). Making technological innovation work for sustainable development. *Proceedings of the National Academy of Sciences, 113*(35), 9682–9690.

Anderson, K. (1987). On why agriculture declines with economic growth. *Agricultural Economics, 1*(3), 195–207.

Andrews, M., Pritchett, L., & Woolcock, M. (2017). *Building State Capability: Evidence, Analysis, Action.* Oxford: Oxford University Press.

Anzolin, G., & Lebdioui, A. (2021). Three dimensions of green industrial policy in the context of climate change and sustainable development. *European Journal of Development Research, 33*, 371–405.

Arrow, K. J. (1972). Economic welfare and the allocation of resources for invention. In C. K. Rowley, ed., *Readings in Industrial Economics.* London: Macmillan Education, pp. 219–236.

Atkin, E. (2018). 'France's Yellow Vest Protesters Want to Fight Climate Change', *The New Republic.* Archived from the original on 11/12/2018. Retrieved 11 December 2018.

Bahn-Walkowiak, B., & Wilts, H. (2017). The institutional dimension of resource efficiency in a multi-level governance system – Implications for policy mix design. *Energy Research & Social Science, 33*, 163–172.

Baldwin, R. & Forslid, R. (2019). Globotics and Development: When Manufacturing Is Jobless and Services Are Tradable. UNU-WIDER Working Paper No. 94/2019. Helsinki: UNU-WIDER

Balsameda, M., Melguizo, A., & Munoz, V. (2022). 'Verde y digital, la simbiosis del futuro', *El País.* 20 December, https://elpais.com/america-futura/2022-12-20/verde-y-digital-la-simbiosis-del-futuro.html.

Barrett, C. B., & Lybbert, T. J. (2000). Is bioprospecting a viable strategy for conserving tropical ecosystems? *Ecological Economics, 34*, 293–300.

Beeson, M. (2010), The coming of environmental authoritarianism, *Environmental Politics, 19*, 276–294.

Behuria, P. (2020). The politics of late late development in renewable energy sectors: Dependency and contradictory tensions in India's National Solar Mission. *World Development, 126*, 104726.

Benson, E. (2023). Beyond Bicycles: A New Momentum behind Environmental Goods Negotiations? www.csis.org/analysis/beyond-bicycles-new-momentum-behind-environmental-goods-negotiations.

Benyus, J. M. (1997). *Biomimicry: Innovation Inspired by Nature.* New York: Morrow.

Breetz, H., Mildenberger, M., & Stokes, L. (2018). The political logics of clean energy transitions. *Business and Politics*, *20*(4), 492–522.

Buhari, M. (2022). 'How not to talk with Africa about climate change'. *Washington Post*. 9 November, www.washingtonpost.com/opinions/2022/11/igerianian-president-cop27-africa-climate-change/.

Buhr, B., Donovan, C., Kling, G., et al. (2018). Climate Change and the Cost of Capital in Developing Countries: Assessing the Impact of Climate Risks on Sovereign Borrowing Costs. *Centre for Climate Finance & Investment, Imperial College Business School, and SOAS, University of London, London.*

Caldecott, B. (2018). *Stranded Assets and the Environment: Risk, Resilience and Opportunity.* Oxford: Routledge.

Campbell, B. M., Thornton, P., Zougmoré, R., Van Asten, P., & Lipper, L. (2014). Sustainable intensification: What is its role in climate smart agriculture? *Current Opinion in Environmental Sustainability*, *8*, 39–43.

Chang, H. C. (2009). Rethinking public policy in agriculture: Lessons from history, distant and recent. *The Journal of Peasant Studies*, *36*(3), 477–515.

Chang, H.-J. (1994). *The Political Economy of Industrial Policy.* Basingstoke: Palgrave Macmillan.

United Nations Industrial Development Organization. (2020). *Industrialization as the Driver of Sustained Prosperity.* Vienna: UNIDO.

Chang, H.-J. (2002). *Kicking Away the Ladder: Development Strategy in Historical Perspective.* London: Anthem Press.

Chang, H. J. (Ed.). (2003). *Rethinking Development Economics.* London: Anthem Press

Chang, H.-J. (2006). Industrial policy in East Asia: Lessons for Europe, EIB Papers, ISSN 0257-7755, European Investment Bank (EIB), Luxembourg, *11*(2), pp. 106–132.

Chang, H.-J. (2011). Industrial policy: Can we go beyond an unproductive confrontation? In *Annual World Bank Conference on Development Economics*. Washington, DC: World Bank, pp. 83–109.

Chang, H.-J., & Lebdioui, A. (2020). *From Fiscal Stabilization to Economic Diversification: A Developmental Approach to Managing Resource Revenues.* WIDER Working Paper No. 2020/108.

Chang, H.-J., & Lebdioui, A., & Albertone, B. (2024). *Decarbonised, Dematerialised, and Developmental: Towards a New Framework for Sustainable Industrialisation.* Geneva: UNCTAD.

Chang, H.-J., Hauge, J., & Irfan, M. (2016). *Transformative Industrial Policy for Africa.* Addis Ababa: United Nations Economic Commission for Africa.

Cherif, R., & Hasanov, F. (2019). *The Return of the Policy That Shall Not Be Named: Principles of Industrial Policy.* International Monetary Fund.

Cimoli, M., Dosi, G., & Stiglitz, J. E. (2009). *Industrial Policy and Development: The Political Economy of Capabilities Accumulation*. New York: Oxford, pp. 113–137

Colenbrander, S., Cao, C., & Pettinotti, L. (2022). *A Fair Share of Climate Finance? An Appraisal of Past Performance, Future Pledges and Prospective Contributors*. London: Overseas Development Institute.

Conway, J. (2020). *Helping Vietnam's Coffee Sector Become More Climate Resilient*. New York: Colombia University. https://news.climate.columbia .edu/2020/11/13/vietnam-coffee-climate-resilient/.

Cramer, C., & Sender, J. (2019). Oranges are not only fruit: The industrialization of freshness and the quality of growth. In A. Noman, J. E. Stiglitz, & R. Kanbur, eds., *The quality of growth in Africa*. New York: Columbia University Press, pp. 209–233.

Davies, R. (1996). Promoting regional integration in africa: an analysis of prospects and problems from a South African perspective. *African Security Review, 5* (5), 109–126.

Dechezleprêtre, A., Martin, R., & Mohnen, M. (2013). *Knowledge spillovers from clean and dirty technologies*. Grantham Research Institute on Climate Change and the Environment (No. 135), Working Paper No. 135.

Dercon, S. (2022). *Gambling on Development*. London: Hurst.

Dikau, S., & Volz, U. (2021). Central bank mandates, sustainability objectives and the promotion of green finance. *Ecological Economics, 184*, 107022.

Eaton, S., & Kostka, G. (2014). Authoritarian environmentalism undermined? Local leaders' time horizons and environmental policy implementation in China. *The China Quarterly, 218*, 359–380.

Eberhard, A., & Naude, R. (2017). The South African Renewable Energy IPP Procurement Programme: Review, Lessons Learned & Proposals to Reduce Transaction Costs, Graduate School of Business, University of Cape Town.

ECLAC. (2022). How to finance sustainable development. Special Report COVID-19 No. 13. Santiago: ECLAC.

Eicher, C. K., & Staatz, J. M. (Eds.). (1998). *International Agricultural Development*. Baltimore: Johns Hopkins University Press.

Ekins, P., & Zenghelis, D. (2021). The costs and benefits of environmental sustainability. *Sustainability Science, 16*, 949–965.

Ellen MacArthur Foundation. (2015). *Towards a Circular Economy: Business Rationale for an Accelerated Transition*. Cowes: Ellen MacArthur Foundation.

Estevez, I. (2023). *Multi-Solving, Trade-Offs, and Conditionalities in Industrial Policy*. Briefs. Washington, DC: Roosevelt Institute.

Evans, P. (1995). *Embedded Autonomy: States and Industrial Transformation*. Princeton: Princeton University Press.

Fermanian Business & Economic Institute. (2015). Bioinspired Innovation: An Economic engine. In C. Smith, A. Bernett, E. Hanson, & C. Garvin, eds., *Tapping into Nature: The Future of Energy, Innovation, and Business*. New York: Terrapin Bright Green LLC, pp. 10–13.

Fermanian Business & Economic Institute. (2020). The Da Vinci China Index: 2000–2019 Report Point. San Diego, CA: Loma Nazarene University.

Ferreira, G. F. C., Fuentes, P. A. G., & Ferreira, J. P. C. (2017). The successes and shortcoming of Costa Rica exports diversification policies. *Background paper to the UNCTAD-FAO Commodities and Development Report*.

Fletcher, R., Dressler, W., Büscher, B., & Anderson, Z. R. (2016). Questioning REDD+ and the future of market-based conservation. *Conservation Biology*, *30*(3), 673–675.

Fouquet, R. (2016). Path dependence in energy systems and economic development. *Nature Energy*, *1*(8), 1–5.

Franzoni, J. M., & Ancochea, D. S. (2013). *Good Jobs and Social Services: How Costa Rica Achieved the Elusive Double Incorporation*. Geneva: United Nations Research Institute for Social Development

Freitag, C., Berners-Lee, M., Widdicks, K., et al. (2021). The real climate and transformative impact of ICT: A critique of estimates, trends, and regulations. *Patterns*, *2*(9), 1–18.

Gollin, D. (2018). Structural Transformation and Growth without Industrialisation, Pathways to Prosperity Commission Background Paper Series No. 2. Oxford: Oxford University Press.

Gabor, D. (2021). The wall street consensus. *Development and Change*, *52*(3), 429–459.

Gabor, D. (2023). The (European) Derisking State. https://doi.org/10.31235/osf.io/hpbj2.

Gabor, D., & Sylla, N. S. (2023). Derisking developmentalism: A tale of green hydrogen. *Development and Change*, *54*: 1169–1196.

Garrett-Peltier, H. (2017). Green versus brown: Comparing the employment impacts of energy efficiency, renewable energy, and fossil fuels using an input-output model. *Economic Modelling*, *61*, 439–447.

Gartner. (2007). Gartner estimates ICT industry accounts for 2 percent of global CO_2 emissions. *Gartner Press Release*. 26 April. https://web.archive.org/web/20070827000406/http://www.gartner.com/it/page.jsp?id=503867.

Gereffi, G. (2019). Economic upgrading in global value chains. In S. Ponte, G. Gereffi, & G. Raj-Reichert, eds., *Handbook on Global Value Chains*. Edward Elgar Publishing. Cheltenham: Edward Elgar Publishing, pp. 240–254

Ghosh, J., Chakraborty, S., & Das, D. (2023). El imperialismo climático en el siglo XXI. *El trimestre económico*, *90*(357), 267–291.

Gilley, B. (2012), Authoritarian environmentalism and China's response to climate change, *Environmental Politics*, *21*, 287–307.

Global Justice Now (2021). Briefing: Corporate courts vs the climate. September 16. Accessible at: https://www.globaljustice.org.uk/resource/cor porate-courts-vs-the-climate-briefing/.

Gore, T. (2020). Confronting carbon inequality. Putting climate justice at the heart of the COVID-19 recovery. Nairobi: OXFAM.

Government of Barbados. (2022). The 2022 Bridgetown Initiative. www.for eign.gov.bb/the-2022-barbados-agenda/.

Guo, J. X., & Fan, Y. (2017). Optimal abatement technology adoption based upon learning-by-doing with spillover effect. *Journal of Cleaner Production*, *143*, 539–548.

Hale, T., Held, D., & Young, K. (2013). *Gridlock: Why Global Cooperation Is Failing When We Need It Most*. London: Polity.

Hallegatte, S., Fay, M., & Vogt-Schilb, A. (2013). Green Industrial Policy: When and How. World Bank Policy Research Working Paper No. 6677. Washington, DC: World Bank.

Hallegatte, S., & Rozenberg, J. (2017). Climate change through a poverty lens. *Nature Climate Change*, *7*(4), 250–256.

Hallegatte, S., Mealy, P., Ganslmeier, M., & Godinho, C. (2024). Empirical Identification of Feasible and Strategic Climate Policies. https://doi.org/ 10.21203/rs.3.rs-3868581/v1.

Hauge, J. (2020). Industrial policy in the era of global value chains: Towards a developmentalist framework drawing on the industrialisation experiences of South Korea and Taiwan. *The World Economy*, *43*(8), 2070–2092.

Hauge, J. (2023). *The Future of the Factory*. Oxford: Oxford University Press.

Heine, J. (2012). Regional integration and political cooperation in Latin America. *Latin American Research Review*, *47*(3), 209–217.

Hess, D. J. (2018). Energy democracy and social movements: A multi-coalition perspective on the politics of sustainability transitions. *Energy Research and Social Science, 40*, 177–189.

Hickel, J. (2020). Quantifying national responsibility for climate breakdown: An equality-based attribution approach for carbon dioxide emissions in excess of the planetary boundary. *The Lancet Planetary Health*, *4*(9), e399–e404.

Hochstetler, K. (2020). *Political Economies of Energy Transition: Wind and Solar Power in Brazil and South Africa*. Cambridge: Cambridge University Press.

Hochstetler, K., & Keck, M. E. (2007). *Greening Brazil: Environmental Activism in State and Society*. Durham: Duke University Press.

Hochstetler, K., & Kostka, G. (2015). Wind and solar power in Brazil and China: Interests, state – business relations, and policy outcomes. *Global Environmental Politics, 15*(3), 74–94.

Hochstetler, K., & Viola, E. (2012). Brazil and the Politics of Climate Change: Beyond the Global Commons. *Environmental Politics, 21*(5), 753–771.

Hübler, M. (2019). How trade in ecotourism services can save nature: A policy scenario analysis. *Development Southern Africa, 36*(1), 127–143.

Humphrey, J., & Schmitz, H. (2000). Global Governance and Upgrading: Linking Industrial Cluster and Global Value Chain Research. IDS Working Paper 120. Brighton: Institute of Development Studies.

Hunt, C. A., Durham, W. H., Driscoll, L., & Honey, M. (2015). Can ecotourism deliver real economic, social, and environmental benefits? A study of the Osa Peninsula, Costa Rica. *Journal of Sustainable Tourism, 23*(3), 339–357.

Hydrogen Council and McKinsey & Company. (2022). *Hydrogen Insights Report September 2022.* https://hydrogencouncil.com/wp-content/uploads/2022/09/Hydrogen-Insights-2022-2.pdf.

IEA, IRENA, UNSD, World Bank and WHO. (2021). *Tracking SDG 7: The Energy Progress Report.* Washington, DC: World Bank.

ILO. (2019). *Advancing Social Justice: Shaping the Future of Work in Africa.* Geneva: International Labour Organization.

Inter-American Development Bank. (2014). *Megacities & Infrastructure in Latin America: What Its People Think.* Washington, DC: Inter-American Development Bank.

International Advisory Council of the Global Bioeconomy Summit. (2018). *Innovation in the Global Bioeconomy for Sustainable and Inclusive Transformation and Wellbeing.* 20 April. Berlin: IACBG.

International Energy Agency – IEA. (2021). *World Energy Outlook.* Paris: IEA.

International Energy Agency – IEA. (2024). *Renewables 2023.* Paris: IEA.

IPCC. (2000). *Methodological and Technological Issues in Technology Transfer.* Cambridge: Cambridge University Press.

IRENA. (2015). *RD&D for Renewable Energy Technologies: Cooperation in Latin America and the Caribbean.* Abu Dhabi: IRENA.

IRENA. (2020). *Renewable Energy and Jobs – Annual Review 2020.* Abu Dhabi: IRENA.

IRENA. (2021). *Renewable Energy and Jobs – Annual Review 2020.* Abu Dhabi: IRENA.

IRENA. (2022). *Geopolitics of the Energy Transformation: The Hydrogen Factor.* Abu Dhabi: IRENA.

IRENA and AfDB. (2022). Renewable Energy Market Analysis: Africa and Its Regions. Abu Dhabi: International Renewable Energy Agency and African Development Bank.

Ismail, F. (2018). A 'developmental regionalism' approach to the AfCFTA. *Celebration of the 90th Birthday of Chief Olu Akinkugbe CFR CON.* Retrieved on 4 November 2021.

Ismail, F. (2022). *Trade and Climate-Resilient Development in Africa: Towards a Global Green New Deal.* Forum on Trade, Environment & the SDGs (TESS).

Jacobson, S. K., & Lopez, A. L. (1994). Biological Impacts of Ecotourism: Tourists and Nesting Turtles in Tortuguero National Park, Costa Rica. *Wildlife Society Bulletin, 22*(3), 414–419.

Kaldor, N. (1967). *Strategic Factors in Economic Development.* Ithaca: New York State School of Industrial and Labor Relations, Cornell University.

Kaufman, M. (2020). The carbon footprint sham. A 'successful, deceptive' PR campaign. *Mashable Social Good Series.*

Kennedy, E., Fecheyr-Lippens, D., Hsiung, B. K., Niewiarowski, P. H., & Kolodziej, M. (2015). Biomimicry: A path to sustainable innovation. *Design Issues, 31*(3), 66–73.

Khan, M. (2010). Political settlements and the governance of growth-enhancing institutions. Research Paper Series on Governance for Growth. London: SOAS, University of London, London. Accessible at http://eprints.soas.ac.uk/9968.

Knight, K. W., Schor, J. B., & Jorgenson, A. K. (2017). Wealth inequality and carbon emissions in high-income countries. Social Currents, *4*(5), 403–412.

Khan, M. J., Ponte, S., & Lund-Thomsen, P. (2020). The 'factory manager dilemma': Purchasing practices and environmental upgrading in apparel global value chains. *Environment and Planning A: Economy and Space, 52*(4), 766–789.

Koens, J. F., Dieperink, C., & Miranda, M. (2009). Ecotourism as a development strategy: Experiences from Costa Rica. *Environment, Development and Sustainability, 11*(6), 1225–1237.

Kostka, G., & Mol, A. P. (2017). Implementation and participation in China's local environmental politics: Challenges and innovations. In G. Kostka & A. P. Mol, eds., *Local Environmental Politics in China.* New York: Routledge, pp. 1–14.

Kvangraven, I. H. (2021). Beyond the stereotype: Restating the relevance of the dependency research programme. Development and Change, 52(1), 76–112.

Lebdioui, A. (2019). Chile's export diversification since 1960: A free market miracle or mirage? *Development and Change, 50*(6), 1624–1663.

Lebdioui, A. (2020). The political economy of moving up in global value chains: How Malaysia added value to its natural resources through industrial policy. *Review of International Political Economy, 29*(3), 870–903.

Lebdioui, A. (2022a). *Latin American Trade in the Age of Climate Change: Impact, Opportunities, and Policy Options*. Canning House: London School of Economics.

Lebdioui, A. (2022b). Nature-inspired innovation policy: Biomimicry as a pathway to leverage biodiversity for economic development. *Ecological Economics*, *202*, 107585.

Lebdioui, A., Lee, K., & Pietrobelli, C. (2021). Local-foreign technology interface, resource-based development, and industrial policy: How Chile and Malaysia are escaping the middle-income trap. *The Journal of Technology Transfer*, *46*, 660–685.

Lee, K. (2013). *Schumpeterian Analysis of Economic Catch-Up, Knowledge, Path-Creation and the Middle-Income Trap*. Cambridge: Cambridge University Press.

Lema, A., & Ruby, K. (2006). Towards a policy model for climate change mitigation: China's experience with wind power development and lessons for developing countries. *Energy for Sustainable Development*, *10*(4), 5–13.

Lema, A., & Ruby, K. (2007). Between fragmented authoritarianism and policy coordination: Creating a Chinese market for wind energy. *Energy Policy*, *35* (7), 3879–3890.

Lema, R., & Lema, A. (2012). Technology transfer? The rise of China and India in green technology sectors. *Innovation and Development*, *2*(1), 23–44.

Lema, R., Iizuka, M., & Walz, R. (2015). Introduction to low-carbon innovation and development: Insights and future challenges for research. *Innovation and Development*, *5*(2), 173–187.

Lema, R., Fu, X., & Rabellotti, R. (2020). Green windows of opportunity: Latecomer development in the age of transformation toward sustainability. *Industrial and Corporate Change*, *29*(5), 1193–1209. https://doi.org/10.1093/icc/dtaa044.

Lema, R. & Perez, C. (2024) The green transformation as a new direction for techno-economic development. UNU-MERIT Working Paper #2024–001. Maastricht: United Nations University, Maastricht Economic and social Research institute on Innovation and Technology.

Lenain, P. (2023). Differentiated carbon prices in the electricity sector: Towards a cooperative approach based on purchasing power parity. OECD Forum. https://www.oecd-forum.org/posts/differentiated-carbon-prices-in-the-electricity-sector-towards-a-cooperative-approach-based-on-purchasing-power-parity.

Li, L. C. (2010). Central-local relations in the people's Republic of China: Trends, processes and impacts for policy implementation. *Public Administration and Development*, *30*(3), 177–190.

Lieberthal, K. G. (1992). Introduction: The 'fragmented authoritarianism' model and its limitations. *Bureaucracy, Politics, and Decision Making in Post-Mao China, 1*, 6–12.

Limb, L. (2022). 'Inside the "secretive" tribunals where fossil fuel companies "steal" from developing countries'. *Euronews*. 19 November.

Lin, J., & Chang, H.-J. (2009). Should industrial policy in developing countries conform to comparative advantage or defy it? A debate between Justin Lin and Ha-Joon Chang. *Development Policy Review, 27*(5), 483–502.

Liu, L., Zhang, B., & Bi, J. (2012). Reforming China's multi-level environmental governance: Lessons from the 11th Five-Year Plan. *Environmental Science & Policy, 21*, 106–111.

Lo, K. (2015). How authoritarian is the environmental governance of China? *Environmental Science & Policy, 54*, 152–159.

Lopes, C. (2022). 'Africa needs to stick to renewables despite the temptation of gas'. *The Africa Report*. www.theafricareport.com/a-message-from/african climatechange/the-africa-climate-conversation/africa-needs-to-stick-to-renewables-despite-the-temptation-of-gas/.

Lourenço, I. C., Callen, J. L., Branco, M. C., & Curto, J. D. (2014). The value relevance of reputation for sustainability leadership. *Journal of Business Ethics, 119*, 17–28.

Lundvall, B. Å. (1999). National business systems and national systems of innovation. *International Studies of Management & Organization, 29*(2), 60–77.

Lundvall, B. Å. (2016). *The Learning Economy and the Economics of Hope*. Anthem Press.

Lütkenhorst, W., Altenburg, T., Pegels, A., & Vidican, G. (2014). 'Green Industrial Policy: Managing Transformation under Uncertainty', *DIE Discussion Paper*. Bonn: Deutsches Institut für Entwicklungspolitik.

MacAskill, S., Roca, E., Liu, B., Stewart, R. A., & Sahin, O. (2021). Is there a green premium in the green bond market? Systematic literature review revealing premium determinants. *Journal of Cleaner Production, 280*, 124491.

Macías Barberán, R., Cuenca Nevárez, G., Intriago Flor, F., et al. (2019). Vulnerability to climate change of smallholder cocoa producers in the province of Manabí, Ecuador. *Revista Facultad Nacional de Agronomía Medellín, 72*(1), 8707–8716.

Mahathir M. (2007). Revisiting vision 2020: New challenges for Malaysia. In A. R. Nungsari and S. A. Suryani, eds., *Readings on Development: Malaysia 2057: Uncommon Voices, Common Aspirations*. Kuala Lumpur: Khazanah Nasional.

Malavasi, E. O., & Kellenberg, J. (2002). Program of payments for ecological services in Costa Rica. In *Building Assets for People and Nature:*

International Expert Meeting on Forest Landscape Restoration. Costa Rica: Heredia, Vol. 27. 1–7.

Malerba, F. (2002). Sectoral systems of innovation and production. *Research Policy, 31*(2), 247–264.

Malik, A. (2019). The political economy of macroeconomic policy in Arab resource-rich economies. In K. Mohaddes, J. B., Nugent, & H. Selim, eds., *Institutions and Macroeconomic Policies in Resource-Rich Arab economies*. Oxford: Oxford University Press, pp. 17–51.

Manley, D., Heller, P. R., & Davis, W. (2022). *No Time to Waste: Governing Cobalt Amid the Energy Transition*. London: Natural Resource Governance Institute.

Marchi, V. D., Maria, E. D., & Micelli, S. (2013). Environmental strategies, upgrading and competitive advantage in global value chains. *Business Strategy and the Environment, 22*(1), 62–72.

Massarella, K., Sallu, S. M., Ensor, J. E., & Marchant, R. (2018). REDD+, hype, hope and disappointment: The dynamics of expectations in conservation and development pilot projects. *World Development, 109*, 375–385.

Mateo, N., Nader, W., & Tamayo, G. (2001). Bioprospecting. *Encyclopedia of Biodiversity, 1*, 471–488.

Mazibuko-Makena, Z., & Kraemer-Mbula, E. (Eds.). (2021). *Leap 4.0. African Perspectives on the Fourth Industrial Revolution: African Perspectives on the Fourth Industrial Revolution*. Johannesburg: African Books Collective.

Mazzucato, M. (2013). *The Entrepreneurial State: Debunking Public vs. Private Sector Myths*. London: Anthem Press.

Mazzucato, M. (2015). The green entrepreneurial state. In B. Scoones, M. Leach, P. Newell (eds). *The Politics of Green Transformations*, London: Routledge. 134–153

Mazzucato, M. (2016). From market fizing to market creating: A new framework for innovation policy. *Industry and Innovation, 23*(2), 140–156.

Mazzucato, M., & Rodrik, D. (2023). Industrial Policy with Conditionalities: A Taxonomy and Sample Cases. *UCL Institute for Innovation and Public Purpose, Working Paper Series* (IIPP WP 2023–07).

Mealy, P., & Teytelboym, A. (2022). Economic complexity and the green economy. *Research Policy, 51*(8), 103948.

Mellor, J. W. (1966). *The Economics of Agricultural Development*. Ithaca, NY: Cornell University Press.

Mellor, J. W. (Eds.). (1995). *Agriculture on the Road to Industrialization*. Baltimore: International Food Policy Research Institute.

Merke, F., Stuenkel, O., & Feldmann, A. E. (2021). Reimagining Regional Governance in Latin America. Carnegie Endowment for International Peace.

https://carnegieendowment.org/2021/06/24/reimagining-regional-govern ance-in-latin-america-pub-84813.

Morris, M., Kaplinsky, R., & Kaplan, D. (2012). 'One thing leads to another' – Commodities, linkages and industrial development. *Resources Policy, 37*(4), 408–416.

Muradian, R., Arsel, M., Pellegrini, L., et al. (2013). Payments for ecosystem services and the fatal attraction of win-win solutions. *Conservation Letters, 6* (4), 274–279.

Mukherjee, P. (2023). Exclusive: South Africa's green power push falters as projects fail. *Reuters*. 18 July. https://www.reuters.com/business/energy/ south-africas-green-power-push-falters-projects-fail-2023-07-18/.

Nayyar, G., Cruz, M., & Zhu, L. (2018). Does Premature Deindustrialization Matter? The Role of Manufacturing and Services in Development. Policy Research Paper No. 8596. Washington, DC: The World Bank.

Nayyar, G., Hallward-Driemeier, M., & Davies, E. (2021). *At Your Service?: The Promise of Services-Led Development*. Washington, DC: The World Bank.

Nelson, D., & Shrimali, G. (2014). Finance mechanisms for lowering the cost of renewable energy in rapidly developing countries. *Climate Policy Initiative*.

Nelson, R. R., & Winter, S. J. (1982). *An Evolutionary Theory of Economic Change*. Cambridge, MA: Harvard University Press.

Newell, P., & Paterson, M. (2010). *Climate Capitalism: Global Warming and the Transformation of the Global Economy*. Cambridge: Cambridge University Press.

Newfarmer, R., Page, J., & Tarp, F. (2019). *Industries without Smokestacks: Industrialization in Africa Reconsidered*. Oxford: Oxford University Press.

Nidumolu, R., Prahalad, C. K., & Rangaswami, M. R. (2009). Why sustainability is now the key driver of innovation. *Harvard Business Review, 87*(9), 56–64.

Nogueira, L. A. H., & Capaz, R. S. (2013). Biofuels in Brazil: Evolution, achievements and perspectives on food security. *Global Food Security, 2* (2), 117–125.

Nordhaus, W. D. (2007). A review of the Stern review on the economics of climate change. *Journal of Economic Literature, 45*(3), 686–702. https://doi .org/10.1257/jel.45.3.686.

Nurkse, R. (1961). International trade theory and development policy. In H. S. Ellis, ed., *Development for Latin America*. New York: St. Martin's Press, pp. 234–263.

Ocampo, J. A. (Ed.). (2006). *Regional Financial Cooperation*. Washington, DC: ECLAC/Brookings Institution Press.

Okereke, C., Coke, A., Geebreyesus, M., et al. (2019). Governing green indus- trialisation in Africa: Assessing key parameters for a sustainable socio-technical transition in the context of Ethiopia. *World Development,* *115,* 279–290.

Oppenheimer, M., Glavovic, B. C., Hinkel, J., et al. (2019). Sea level rise and implications for low-lying islands, coasts and communities. In *IPCC Special Report on the Ocean and Cryosphere in a Changing Climate.* Cambridge: Cambridge University Press, pp. 321–445.

Overman, H., Butt, N., Cummings, A. R., Luzar, J. B., & Fragoso, J. M. (2018). National REDD+ implications for tenured indigenous communities in Guyana, and communities' impact on forest carbon stocks. *Forests, 9*(5), 231.

Overman, H., Cummings, A. R., Luzar, J. B., & Fragoso, J. M. (2019). National REDD outcompetes gold and logging: The potential of cleaning profit chains. *World Development, 118,* 16–26.

Oyemitan, I. A. (2017). African medicinal spices of genus *Piper.* In V. Kuete, Ed., *Medicinal Spices and Vegetables from Africa.* Academic Press, pp. 581–597.

Pack, H., & Saggi, K. (2006). Is there a case for industrial policy? A critical survey. *The World Bank Research Observer, 21*(2), 267–297.

Palage, K., Lundmark, R., & Söderholm, P. (2019). The innovation effects of renewable energy policies and their interaction: The case of solar photovoltaics. *Environmental Economics and Policy Studies, 21,* 217–254.

Palmer, R. (2017). *Jobs and Skills Mismatch in the Informal Economy.* Geneva: International Labour Organisation.

Palombi, L., & Sessa, R. (2013). *Climate-Smart Agriculture: Sourcebook.* Food and Agriculture Organization of the United Nations (FAO).

Parente, R., Melo, M., Andrews, D., Kumaraswamy, A., & Vasconcelos, F. (2021). Public sector organizations and agricultural catch-up dilemma in emerging markets: The orchestrating role of Embrapa in Brazil. *Journal of International Business Studies, 52,* 646–670.

Park, A. S. (2023). Understanding resilience in sustainable development: Rallying call or siren song? *Sustainable Development.*

Pearce, D. W., & Pearce, C. (2001). The Value of Forest Ecosystems, Report to the Convention on Biological Diversity, Toronto.

Pegels, A. (Ed.). (2014). *Green Industrial Policy in Emerging Countries.* London: Routledge.

Pegels, A., & Altenburg, T. (2020). Latecomer development in a 'greening' world: Introduction to the Special Issue. *World Development, 135,* 105084.

Perez, C. (2010). Technological dynamism and social inclusion in Latin America: A resource-based production development strategy. CEPAL Review No. 100, pp. 121–141.

Perez, C. (2016). Capitalism, technology and a green global golden age: The role of history in helping to shape the future. In M. Jacobs & M. Mazzucato, eds., *Rethinking Capitalism: Economics and Policy for Sustainable and Inclusive Growth*. London: Wiley Blackwell, Vol. 1, pp. 191–217.

Pietrobelli, C., & Seri, C. (2023). Reshoring, nearshoring and development: Readiness and implications for Latin America and the Caribbean. *Transnational Corporations Journal, 30*(2). 37–70.

Ponte, S. (2019). *Business, Power and Sustainability in a World of Global Value Chains*. London: Bloomsbury.

Prebisch, R. (1950). *The Economic Development of Latin America and Its Principal Problems*. Santiago: UN Economic Comission for Latin America.

Radley, B. (2023). Green imperialism, sovereignty, and the quest for national development in the Congo. *Review of African Political Economy, 50*, 177–178, 322–339.

Reich, R. (1982). Why the U.S. Needs an Industrial Policy. Harvard Business Review. January, https://hbr.org/1982/01/why-the-us-needs-an-industrial-policy.

Riofrancos, T., Kendall, A., Dayemo, K. K., et al. (2023). Achieving zero emissions with more mobility and less mining. *Climate and community project.*

Ritchie, H. (2021). How much of global greenhouse gas emissions come from food? *Our World in Data.* 18 March. https://ourworldindata.org/greenhouse-gas-emissions-food.

Rodrik, D. (2004). Industrial policy for the twenty-first century. Available at SSRN 666808. Accessible at: https://drodrik.scholar.harvard.edu/files/dani-rodrik/files/industrial-policy-twenty-first-century.pdf.

Rodrik, D. (2014). Green Industrial Policy. *Oxford Review of Economic Policy, 30*(3), pp.469–491.

Rogge, K. S., Kern, F., & Howlett, M. (2017). Conceptual and empirical advances in analysing policy mixes for energy transitions. *Energy Research & Social Science, 33*, 1–10.

Romero, J. P., & Gramkow, C. (2021). Economic complexity and greenhouse gas emissions. *World Development, 139*, 105317.

Rosenberg, N. (1976). On technological expectations. *The Economic Journal, 86*(343), 523–535.

Saget, C., Vogt-Schilb, A., & Luu, T. (2020). *Jobs in a Net-Zero Emissions Future in Latin America and the Caribbean*. Geneva: Inter-American Development Bank and International Labour Organization.

Salazar-Xirinachs, J. M. (1993). The role of the state and the market in economic development. In O. Sunkel, ed., *Development from Within: Toward a Neostructuralist Approach for Latin America*. Boulder, CO: Lynne Rienner, pp. 359–396.

Salazar-Xirinachs, J. M. (2002). Proliferation of sub-regional trade agreements in the Americas: An assessment of key analytical and policy issues. *Journal of Asian Economics, 13*(2), 181–212.

Schmidt, T. S. (2014). Low-carbon investment risks and de-risking. *Nature Climate Change, 4*(4), 237–239.

Schultz, T. W. (1968). *Economic Growth and Agriculture*. London: McGraw-Hill.

Semieniuk, G., & Yakovenko, V. M. (2020). Historical evolution of global inequality in carbon emissions and footprints versus redistributive scenarios. *Journal of Cleaner Production, 264*, 121420.

Semieniuk, G., Campiglio, E., Mercure, J. F., Volz, U., & Edwards, N. R. (2021). Low-carbon transition risks for finance. *Wiley Interdisciplinary Reviews: Climate Change, 12*(1), e678.

Sen, K. (2023). *Varieties of Structural Transformation: Patterns, Determinants, and Consequences*. Cambridge: Cambridge University Press.

Shen, W., & Xie, L. (2017). The political economy for low-carbon energy transition in China: towards a new policy paradigm?. *New Political Economy, 23*(4), 407–421.

Sierra, R., & Russman, E. (2006). On the efficiency of environmental service payments: A forest conservation assessment in the Osa Peninsula, Costa Rica. *Ecological Economics, 59*(1), 131–141.

Simpson, R. D., Sedjo, R. A., & Reid, J. W. (1996). Valuing biodiversity for use in pharmaceutical research. *Journal of Political Economy, 104*(1), 163–185.

Singer, H. W. (1950). The Distribution of Gains between Investing and Borrowing Countries, *The American Economic Review* 40.2: 473–485.

Smith, S., & Braathen, N. A. (2015). *Monetary Carbon Values in Policy Appraisal: An Overview of Current Practice and Key Issues*. Paris: OECD.

Soto, D., León-Muñoz, J., Dresdner, J., et al. (2019). Salmon farming vulnerability to climate change in southern Chile: Understanding the biophysical, socio-economic and governance links. *Reviews in Aquaculture, 11*(2), 354–374.

Soulé, F. (2023). What a U.S.-DRC-Zambia Electric Vehicle Batteries Deal Reveals about the New U.S. Approach toward Africa. https://carnegieendow ment.org/2023/08/21/what-u.s.-drc-zambia-electric-vehicle-batteries-deal-reveals-about-new-u.s.-approach-toward-africa-pub-90383.

Sovacool, B. K., Martiskainen, M., Hook, A., & Baker, L. (2020). Beyond cost and carbon: The multidimensional co-benefits of low carbon transitions in Europe. *Ecological Economics, 169*, 106529.

Steffen, B. (2020). Estimating the cost of capital for renewable energy projects. *Energy Economics, 88*, 104783.

Stem, C. J., Lassoie, J. P., Lee, D. R., & Deshler, D. J. (2003). How eco is ecotourism? A comparative case study of ecotourism in Costa Rica. *Journal of Sustainable Tourism*, *11*(4), 322–347.

Stern, N. H. (2007). *The Economics of Climate Change: The Stern Review.* Cambridge: Cambridge University Press.

Stiglitz, J. (2015). Overcoming the Copenhagen failure with flexible commitments. *Economics of Energy and Environmental Policy*, *4*(2). 29–36.

Stiglitz, S. (2016). *The Euro and Its Threat to the Future of Europe*. London: Penguin Random House.

Stoneman, P. (1983). *The Economic Analysis of Technological Change*. Oxford: Oxford University Press.

Studwell, J. (2013). How Asia works: Success and failure in the world's most dynamic region. Open Road+ Grove/Atlantic.

Swanson, T. (1996). The reliance of northern economies on southern biodiversity: Biodiversity as information. *Ecological Economics*, *17*(1), 1–8.

Szklo, A. S., Schaeffer, R., Schuller, M. E., & Chandler, W. (2005). Brazilian energy policies side-effects on CO2 emissions reduction. *Energy Policy*, *33*(3), 349–364.

The Guardian. (2011). 'Bank reforms: How much did we bail them out and how much do they still owe?'. www.theguardian.com/news/datablog/2011/nov/12/bank-bailouts-uk-credit-crunch.

Tienhaara, K. (2018). Regulatory chill in a warming world: the threat to climate policy posed by Investor-State Dispute Settlement. *Transnational environmental law*, 7(2), 229–250.

Timperley, J. (2021). The broken $100-billion promise of climate finance – and how to fix it. *Nature*, *598*(7881), 400–402.

Trumbull, R. (1982). World's richest little isle. *New York Times*. 7 March. https://www.nytimes.com/1982/03/07/magazine/world-s-richest-little-isle.html.

Tucker, T. N., & Meyer, T. (2022). Reshaping global trade and investment law for a Green New Deal. In Tienhaara, K., & Robinson, J. (Eds.). (2022). Routledge Handbook on the Green New Deal. London: Taylor & Francis.

UNCTAD (2013). *Economic Development Report*. Geneva: United Nations

UNCTAD. (2019). *State of Commodity Dependence 2019*. Geneva: United Nations.

UNCTAD (2023) *State of Commodity Dependence 2019*. Geneva: United Nations.

UNDP. (2013). *Derisking Renewable Energy Investment*. New York: United Nations.

UNESCO. (2022). *Recommendation on the Ethics of Artificial Intelligence*. Paris: UNESCO.

US Department of Energy. (2022). *America's Strategy to Secure the Supply Chain for a Robust Clean Energy Transition*. 24 February. Washington, DC : US Department of Energy

US Department of the Treasury (2016). 'Troubled Asset Relief Program". Accessible at https://home.treasury.gov/data/troubled-asset-relief-program.

US Department of the Treasury. (2023). *Bank Investment Programs*. https://home .treasury.gov/data/troubled-assets-relief-program/bank-investment-programs.

Usman, Z. (2023). 'The World Bank Must Do More with Less'. *Foreign Policy*. 29 March.

Usman, Z., Abimbola, O., & Ituen, I. (2021). What does the European green deal mean for Africa?. *Carnegie Endowment for International Peace*. https:// carnegieendowment.org/2021/10/18/what-does-european-green-deal-mean-for-africa-pub-85570.

van Asten, P. J., Wairegi, L. W. I., Mukasa, D., & Uringi, N. O. (2011). Agronomic and economic benefits of coffee–banana intercropping in Uganda's smallholder farming systems. *Agricultural Systems*, *104*(4), 326–334.

van der Ploeg, F., & Rezai, A. (2020). Stranded assets in the transition to a carbon-free economy. *Annual Review of Resource Economics*, *12*(1). 281–298.

Vergara, W., Rios, A. R., Paliza, L. M. G., et al. (2013). *The Climate and Development Challenge for Latin America and the Caribbean: Options for Climate-Resilient, Low-Carbon Development*. Washington, DC: Inter-American Development Bank.

Vieira, H. (2017). Low-carbon services can enhance the UK's economic prospects. *LSE blogs*. 28 August.

Viner, J. (1950). Full employment at whatever cost. *The Quarterly Journal of Economics*, *64*(3), 385–407.`

Viteri Andrade, A. (2019). *Impacto económico y laboral del retiro y/o reconversión de unidades a carbón en Chile* (Estudio desarrollado para el Ministerio de Energía de Chile).

Vogt-Schilb, A., & Feng, K. (2019). *The Labor Impact of Coal Phase Down Scenarios in Chile*. Washington, DC: Inter-American Development Bank.

Volz, U., & Aitken, D. (2022). Public Debt in the Time of COVID-19 and the Climate Crisis. *Background Paper for the Financing for Sustainable Development Report 2022*. New York: United Nations.

Wade, R. (1990). Industrial policy in East Asia: Does it lead or follow the market? In G. Gereffi and D. L. Wyman, eds., *Manufacturing Miracles: Paths of Industrialization in Latin America and East Asia*. Princeton: Princeton University Press, pp. 231–266.

Weitzman, M. L. (1992). On diversity. *The Quarterly Journal of Economics*, *107*(2), 363–405.

Weitzman, M. L. (2007). A review of the Stern Review on the economics of climate change. *Journal of Economic Literature, 45*(3), 703–724.

White House. (2023). Remarks by National Security Advisor Jake Sullivan on Renewing American Economic Leadership at the Brookings Institution. Speeches and Remarks. 27 April.

WTO (2016). India – Certain Measures Relating to Solar Cells and Solar Modules. Report of the Panel Wt/Ds456/R. Geneva: World Trade Organisation.

World Bank. (2017). *The Growing Role of Minerals and Metals for a Low Carbon Future.* Washington, DC: World Bank.

World Bank. (2022). *Poverty and Shared Prosperity 2022: Correcting Course.* Washington, DC: The World Bank.

World Bank. (2023). *World Development Indicators.* https://databank.world bank.org/source/world-development-indicators.

World Bank Enterprise Surveys. (2023). https://www.enterprisesurveys.org/en/ enterprisesurveys .

World Meteorological Organization. (2021a). *State of the Climate in Africa 2020.* Geneva: WMO.

World Meteorological Organization. (2021b). *State of the Climate in Latin America and the Caribbean 2020.* Geneva: WMO.

Wu, M., & Salzman, J. (2014). The next generation of trade and environment conflicts: The rise of green industrial policy. *Northwestern University Law Review, 108*, 401–474.

Zenghelis, D. (2016). 10. Decarbonisation: Innovation and the economics of climate change. *The Political Quarterly, 86*, 172–190.

Acknowledgements

This short book has benefited from the guidance and comments of a large group of people. I am particularly grateful to Tony Addison (for encouraging me to write this book in the first place), Ha-Joon Chang (for his never-failing mentorship), and Carlota Perez (for thought-provoking conversations that have shaped this book's messages).

This book also largely benefited from conversations with – and comments from- various scholars, but also several practitioners, which has helped me better understand the reality on the ground. Therefore, I offer my special thanks to Adriana Abdenur, Andres Valenciano, Angel Melguizo, Arkebe Oqubay, Azman Mokhtar, Baptiste Albertone, Carlo Pietrobelli, Carlos Lopes, Chris Cramer, Chris Hope, Clovis Freire, Evelyn Dietsche, Faten Aggad, Flavien Moreau, Gregor Semieniuk, Isabel Estevez, Jan Yves Remy, Jonathan Di John, Jorge Bula, Jostein Hauge, Kathy Hochstetler, Marcela Morales, Maria Fernanda Valdes, Matthieu Barral, Meriem Ait Ali Slimane, Nik Haukohl, Pavel Bilek, Rasmus Lema, Reda Cherif, Riad Meddeb, Saleha Malik, Sebastian Manhart, Stefan Hobl, Stephane Hallegatte, Ulrich Volz, Zainab Usman and many others.

I am also grateful to the participants of the presentations of this work given at the Harvard Kennedy School, UNCTAD, UNU-WIDER, UNU-MERIT, SOAS, University of London, the World Bank and the International Monetary Fund for valuable feedback and suggestions. Any remaining error is my own.

Last but not least, many thanks to my family, for always being supportive in my endeavours (and especially my sister Mina, for leading by example and whose novels are much nicer to read than this manuscript).

Cambridge Elements ☰

Development Economics

Series Editor-in-Chief
Kunal Sen
UNU-WIDER and University of Manchester

Kunal Sen, UNU-WIDER Director, is Editor-in-Chief of the Cambridge Elements in Development Economics series. Professor Sen has over three decades of experience in academic and applied development economics research, and has carried out extensive work on international finance, the political economy of inclusive growth, the dynamics of poverty, social exclusion, female labour force participation, and the informal sector in developing economies. His research has focused on India, East Asia, and sub-Saharan Africa.

In addition to his work as Professor of Development Economics at the University of Manchester, Kunal has been the Joint Research Director of the Effective States and Inclusive Development (ESID) Research Centre, and a Research Fellow at the Institute for Labor Economics (IZA). He has also served in advisory roles with national governments and bilateral and multilateral development agencies, including the UK's Department for International Development, Asian Development Bank, and the International Development Research Centre.

Thematic Editors
Tony Addison
University of Copenhagen and UNU-WIDER

Tony Addison is a Professor of Economics in the University of Copenhagen's Development Economics Research Group. He is also a Non-Resident Senior Research Fellow at UNU-WIDER, Helsinki, where he was previously the Chief Economist-Deputy Director. In addition, he is Professor of Development Studies at the University of Manchester. His research interests focus on the extractive industries, energy transition, and macroeconomic policy for development.

Chris Barret
Johnson College of Business, Cornell University

Chris Barrett is an agricultural and development economist at Cornell University. He is the Stephen B. and Janice G. Ashley Professor of Applied Economics and Management; and International Professor of Agriculture at the Charles H. Dyson School of Applied Economics and Management. He is also an elected Fellow of the American Association for the Advancement of Science, the Agricultural and Applied Economics Association, and the African Association of Agricultural Economists.

Carlos Gradín
University of Vigo

Carlos Gradín is a professor of applied economics at the University of Vigo. His main research interest is the study of inequalities, with special attention to those that exist between population groups e.g., by race or sex). His publications have contributed to improving the empirical evidence in developing and developed countries, as well as globally, and to improving the available data and methods used.

Rachel M. Gisselquist
UNU-WIDER

Rachel M. Gisselquist is a Senior Research Fellow and member of the Senior Management Team of UNU-WIDER. She specializes in the comparative politics of developing countries, with particular attention to issues of inequality, ethnic and identity politics, foreign aid and state building, democracy and governance, and sub-Saharan African politics. Dr Gisselquist has edited a dozen collections in these areas, and her articles are published in a range of leading journals.

Shareen Joshi
Georgetown University

Shareen Joshi is an Associate Professor of International Development at Georgetown University's School of Foreign Service in the United States. Her research focuses on issues of inequality, human capital investment and grassroots collective action in South Asia. Her work has been published in the fields of development economics, population studies, environmental studies and gender studies.

Patricia Justino
UNU-WIDER and IDS – UK

Patricia Justino is a Senior Research Fellow at UNU-WIDER and Professorial Fellow at the Institute of Development Studies (IDS) (on leave). Her research focuses on the relationship between political violence, governance and development outcomes. She has published widely in the fields of development economics and political economy and is the co-founder and co-director of the Households in Conflict Network (HiCN).

Marinella Leone
University of Pavia

Marinella Leone is an assistant professor at the Department of Economics and Management, University of Pavia, Italy. She is an applied development economist. Her more recent research focuses on the study of early child development parenting programmes, on education, and gender-based violence. In previous research she investigated the short-, long-term and intergenerational impact of conflicts on health, education and domestic violence. She has published in top journals in economics and development economics.

Jukka Pirttilä
University of Helsinki and UNU-WIDER

Jukka Pirttilä is Professor of Public Economics at the University of Helsinki and VATT Institute for Economic Research. He is also a Non-Resident Senior Research Fellow at UNU-WIDER. His research focuses on tax policy, especially for developing countries. He is a co-principal investigator at the Finnish Centre of Excellence in Tax Systems Research.

Andy Sumner
King's College London and UNU-WIDER

Andy Sumner is Professor of International Development at King's College London; a Non-Resident Senior Fellow at UNU-WIDER and a Fellow of the Academy of Social Sciences. He has published extensively in the areas of poverty, inequality, and economic development.

About the Series

Cambridge Elements in Development Economics is led by UNU-WIDER in partnership with Cambridge University Press. The series publishes authoritative studies on important topics in the field covering both micro and macro aspects of development economics.

United Nations University World Institute for Development Economics Research

United Nations University World Institute for Development Economics Research (UNU-WIDER) provides economic analysis and policy advice aiming to promote sustainable and equitable development for all. The institute began operations in 1985 in Helsinki, Finland, as the first research centre of the United Nations University. Today, it is one of the world's leading development economics think tanks, working closely with a vast network of academic researchers and policy makers, mostly based in the Global South.

Cambridge Elements $\equiv$

Development Economics

Elements in the Series

The 1918–20 Influenza Pandemic: A Retrospective in the Time of COVID-19
Prema-chandra Athukorala and Chaturica Athukorala

Parental Investments and Children's Human Capital in Low-to-Middle-Income Countries
Jere R. Behrman

Great Gatsby and the Global South: Intergenerational Mobility, Income Inequality, and Development
Diding Sakri, Andy Sumner and Arief Anshory Yusuf

Varieties of Structural Transformation: Patterns, Determinants, and Consequences
Kunal Sen

Economic Transformation and Income Distribution in China over Three Decades
Cai Meng, Bjorn Gustafsson and John Knight

Chilean Economic Development under Neoliberalism: Structural Transformation, High Inequality and Environmental Fragility
Andrés Solimano and Gabriela Zapata-Román

Hierarchy of Needs and the Measurement of Poverty and Standards of Living
Joseph Deutsch and Jacques Silber

New Structural Financial Economics: A Framework for Rethinking the Role of Finance in Serving the Real Economy
Justin Yifu Lin, Jiajun Xu, Zirong Yang and Yilin Zhang

Knowledge and Global Inequality Since 1800: Interrogating the Present as History
Dev Nathan

Survival of the Greenest: Economic Transformation in a Climate-conscious World
Amir Lebdioui

A full series listing is available at: www.cambridge.org/CEDE

Printed in the United States
by Baker & Taylor Publisher Services